Incredible Insights from

Well-Known Moms and Dads

The Best Advice
I Ever Got on

Compiled by **Jim Daly**

PRESIDENT & CEO OF **FOCUS ON THE FAMILY**

WORTHY
PUBLISHING

FOCUS
ON THE FAMILY

Library of Congress Control Number: 2012946064

ISBN: 978-1-936034-48-2 (hardcover w/ jacket)

Editor: Marianne Hering
Cover Design: Christopher Tobias
Cover Image: © istockphoto.com

Printed in the United States of America

12 13 14 15 16 17 RRD 8 7 6 5 4 3 2 1

INTRODUCTION
Jim Daly

For the first thirty-nine years of my life, I was a detached observer of the parenting scene, even though for much of that time I worked for a Christian family ministry! Not yet being a father, I wasn't especially motivated to absorb every tip and lesson on how best to raise the next generation of children. And, to be honest, I probably assumed I was ready—more or less—to be a father if the Lord so willed it.

And on August 12, 2000, I did become an active participant in the parenting scene. If I close my eyes, I can still see the hospital room and feel the excitement of the big moment. Trent arrived on that golden summer day, and my wife, Jean, and I were thrilled beyond words.

Imagine! Me, a dad! Having been abandoned by my father, I was determined to be everything he wasn't, but I was not entirely sure how I would pull it off.

I began eagerly absorbing every bit of wise parenting counsel I could find. I read the classic books on parenting. I listened more closely to the Focus on the Family Daily Broadcast. I talked with my friends and observed with great interest the admirable parents around me. Parenting was no longer a theoretical exercise: I was a father. And I was determined to be a good one.

How have I done? Like everyone else, I'm still a work in progress.

As I'll share in a minute, the "best advice I ever learned" did not come from the terrific influences and influencers around me. I didn't read it in a book or hear it in a broadcast or from a friend. I learned it years before from my mom.

OWN YOUR MISTAKES

The arrival of your first child is a reflective season of life. There is the sheer wonder of it all, of course, but many parents also tend to wander back in memory to their own childhood. I was one of those. After Trent was born, I found myself looking back and trying to glean some insight from my tumultuous childhood days in Southern California.

My father walked out on my family in the mid-1960s, and my mother became my rock. She was the one person I could depend on. She modeled for me the importance of a parent keeping his or her word. But she taught me so much more, including one lesson I'll never forget.

As a single mother, she had her hands full. Put bluntly, I was a bratty kid, and I probably acted out on several occasions for lack of a father figure. However, one particular incident stands out in my mind above all the others.

My family never had much money, but I grew accustomed to receiving a little toy each time my mother and I went to Crawford's Grocery and Department Store in Alhambra, California. The routine was always the same. She and I would start shopping, and a few minutes into the visit, Mom would

CONTENTS

let me walk over to the toy aisle to do my shopping. I looked forward to that treat, but I came to expect it too. Before I scampered off, she always assured me that she'd stay where she was, allaying any fear that I wouldn't be able to find her upon my return.

On this particular Saturday my mom was shucking corn over in the produce section. After happily picking out my G.I. Joe outfit across the store, I began walking back toward the corn. Suddenly I saw her standing with her back to me in a different aisle. For some inexplicable reason, my young mind couldn't handle it. My mother had lied to me! I flew into a fit of rage. Charging down the aisle toward her, I clenched my right hand and formed a fist. Angry and out of control, I lunged toward her and planted my fist in the small of her back. A hollow thud echoed in the air, and my mother stumbled forward in a daze.

Only it wasn't my mother.

It just so happened that this particular woman was wearing an outfit identical to my mom's. In shock, the stranger twirled around. Looking up, I stammered and mumbled and slowly backed away—and then took off in search of my mom.

When I found her, she was exactly where she told me she'd be. Noticing my tears, she asked what was wrong.

"I just hit a lady."

"Why in the world . . .?"

"Because I thought it was you."

Mom didn't waste time asking questions. She grabbed my collar and dragged me back to the scene of the crime. By now the other woman had composed herself and was again shopping. Mom and I spotted her at the end of an aisle.

My mother stopped moving. "You will apologize to that woman!" she thundered.

I dragged my little feet along the linoleum floor and down the aisle. When I reached my victim, I looked up at her and cleared my throat, shuffling nervously from side to side, wanting to talk but struggling to get the words out. Biting my lip and fighting back tears, I offered an apology. Understandably, my words fell flat. She glared down at me. After I was done talking, this bewildered lady twirled around and muttered something under her breath. Looking back now, I don't blame her. She was rightfully miffed. I can only imagine what she was thinking.

My mother taught me a valuable lesson—some "best advice"—in the peanut butter aisle of Crawford's Grocery. I've attempted to pass on this wisdom to my sons, Trent and Troy: Own your mistake. Admit it. Apologize. And try to right the wrong.

FORTY-FIVE YEARS LATER

Washington, DC, is a long way from Crawford's. But on a recent trip east with Jean and our two boys, I found myself incorporating into my parenting that painful childhood lesson learned in that California store many years ago.

It's always hard to travel with kids, and Jean and I are usually careful not to overschedule. This day, however, was during cherry blossom season, and there were lines of people everywhere. The combination of crowds and our earlier airplane flights had the boys running (flying!) on fumes.

As we worked our way through the International Spy Museum, Trent and Troy were rambunctious, poking at each other and wrestling playfully. I cautioned them to cool it out of respect for the other people in line. But if something interested them, they thoughtlessly though innocently kept jumping ahead and cutting people off or nearly knocking them over. Each time the boys did something like this, I pulled them aside to talk.

"That's entirely unacceptable," I would say to them. "We're raising gentlemen, not barbarians. We don't treat people like that. We wait our turn and respect other people's space. Please go and apologize."

Each time they turned to find their "victims," my mind flashed back forty-five years. What they had done wasn't nearly as offensive as what I had done inside Crawford's Grocery and Department Store. In fact, the boys' actions were only minor infractions by comparison. Their behavior, however, was still unacceptable and needed to be addressed.

Fortunately, each of the people they spoke to accepted their apology warmly. All was forgiven. By the end of the long day, I hoped that a seed had been planted inside their minds—a seed that likely would take many years to germinate and bear fruit.

As my mother had taught me, I was teaching them: Own your mistake. Admit it. Apologize. And try to right the wrong.

TAKE THE LONG VIEW

It's my prayer that you'll embrace your role as a mom or dad with enthusiasm and delight. It's easy to be overwhelmed by the tasks before you and even grow weary of the challenges. Implied within a book of "best advice" is the fact that you'll encounter problems along the way. It's true. Parenthood is not easy, but it's the most significant and rewarding assignment in life. As you read through this collection of parental wisdom, I encourage you to take a long-view perspective. If you are struggling, don't allow your present circumstances to inordinately weigh you down. I have discovered that the best way to calmly handle my role as a father is to gratefully embrace the present and look ahead to other days, knowing full well the brevity of this time.

When I'm old and gray and the boys are grown and gone, the memories of their happy laughter and this innocent era will echo in my heart. But will I be able to look back with a sense of peace and joy? Or will I have regrets and find myself wondering what could have been? It strikes me that the key to living a regret-free life is often found in one's ability to see the end at the beginning.

When our house becomes quiet and tidy, and the curtain falls on my job of intense day-to-day parenting, what will I remember about these days? If you're a parent, what will you recall? Here are some of the things I'll remember . . .

Hearing the boys' first cries and tightly holding newborn Trent and Troy, scared to death that I would drop them, but knowing I never would . . . Late-night drives around a dark neighborhood to soothe a colicky baby . . .

First steps, first words, and midnight toy-assembly jobs on Christmas Eve . . . The pain of leaving on long ministry trips to faraway places—and the joy of reunions at home . . . Vacations on a tight budget—cold and wet tents, cars and trailers that wouldn't run, and kids that wouldn't stop . . .

Skinned knees, bloody noses, and a cell-phone call about a DVD player that had caught on fire . . . Teaching my boys how to fish . . . Jumping on the trampoline, riding bikes, playing tag in a dark house . . . Ballgames and board games . . .

And, best of all, seeing their eyes light up and their hearts open up to the reality of the gospel and to the truth about the life and resurrection of Jesus Christ.

These are only some of the memories that time won't erase . . . because, in the end, these are among the few things that will really matter.

To be sure, I've made my share of mistakes as a dad. But by the grace of God, I can say that I love being a father. I've found myself captivated by my boys. I love spending time with them. I love the way they surprise me with their observations about life. I love wrapping my arms around them when I come home from work.

And I especially cherish their smiles.

No matter how crazy the world seems to get, no matter how hard my day at the office might have been, whenever I look at Trent's and Troy's beaming faces, I can't help but thank God for His goodness to me.

It's the best feeling in the world.

Would it surprise you if I suggested there's really nothing new about parenting inside this book?

It's true.

Oh, there are entertaining characters sharing some pretty unique stories about their personal experiences as a mom or dad.

Many of them will make you laugh. Some will make you cry. And others will leave you in a very thoughtful and reflective mood.

All of them are designed to help you become a better parent.

When I arrived at Focus on the Family over twenty years ago, I appreciated the humility with which our founder, Dr. James Dobson, presented the source of his advice to parents. A journalist might come on campus for a visit, and he or she would try and find out just where Dr. Dobson came up with his ideas—and why the people who read his books and listened to the radio program enthusiastically embraced the concepts. Some of those who analyzed his material thought he was being clever or creative or even original. In the end, Dr. Dobson always tried to give credit where credit was due.

The advice Dr. Dobson offered didn't come from him—he said it came from the Book of books. It came from the Bible.

And so it is with this new offering. I respect, admire, and appreciate the individuals who have contributed to this great project. The stories are all a bit different, but the advice we've culled from them is rooted in the timeless principles found inside the Bible. The authors have done a wonderful job of boiling down a lifetime of perspective to just a few short pages.

I hope you'll find the advice that's tucked away in this book to be as useful and practical and timeless as I have.

July 31, 2012

1

Parenting with Grace

Tim and Darcy Kimmel

Sometimes the best advice we get isn't about what *to* do, but rather what *not* to do.

Picture this: You're sitting in church with your family. The pianist is playing some quiet background music. The senior pastor and worship leader are in a side room just off the platform. Both have on their wireless microphones, but there are three things these men don't realize:

1. Their microphones are hot.

2. The techie who's supposed to be manning the sound booth is nowhere to be found.

3. The volume on their microphones is turned up.

What you overhear goes something like this: light banter . . . some final instructions . . . then one of them making a critical observation about the other. That person fires back a caustic putdown. This is trumped by a toxic insult, accented with profanity. The best you can figure, it sounds like it's the senior pastor who makes the first physically aggressive move—shoving the worship leader into a wall. The worship leader responds with a haymaker that drops the pastor to his knees. Not to be outdone, your dear, sweet pastor lunges forward, toppling the worship leader to the floor, and then you listen in as these two pillars of your church cuss, bite, kick, punch, and knee each other into oblivion.

Meanwhile, the pianist plays on.

Finally, some big guys from the choir head through the door, pull the two apart, calm them down, and help them quickly put their disheveled clothing and hair back into place. The side door opens . . . and the pastor and worship leader enter as if nothing had happened. The pastor peeks inside his Bible to make a quick, last-minute review of his sermon notes as the worship leader moves to the podium, inviting the congregation to join voices in a powerful song of praise to God.

So, what's your next move? Most likely, you look around the auditorium and count your options. There are six of them. Exit signs, that is. So you grab your Bible, pick the closest exit, and head through it as quickly as possible—refusing to look back. One thing's certain: you never, ever want to hear another spiritual insight from these two men again.

OUR EXPECTATIONS

"But," you may ask, "can't pastors have a bad day?" Of course they can, but this was more than a slip of the tongue or a flare of temper. "But," you might then point out, "this is one of the best worship and teaching teams in our community. They always draw a crowd." You may attempt to rationalize their behavior based on their crowd appeal, but your kids—ex officio members of the postmodern "Don't tell me; show me" generation—will have nothing of it.

The most important reason why these men had, with their words and actions, discredited themselves and forfeited their right to be heard is the role they play in the lives of their congregation. They're in a "character profession." People don't hold the same measuring stick up to pastors, worship leaders, lay leaders, and missionaries that they use for almost everyone else. Instead, these people lift up the Bible and proclaim, "Thus sayeth the Lord." Church members know their leaders aren't perfect and don't expect them to be. But church members very much expect their leaders to generally live according to what they teach and what they say they stand for. Such is the cost of being in a character profession.

THE CONNECTION BETWEEN FAITH AND PRACTICE

Well, guess what? Parenting is also a character profession!

Dads and moms are the pastors of the smallest churches out there. In fact, the best definition we've ever heard for a family is "the domestic church." If you are a follower of Jesus, you're a point person for your kids. You hold up the Bible for them, and throughout their childhood, you say, "Thus sayeth the Lord." Your kids know you're not perfect (hey, they live with you!), but your kids do expect you to generally live according to what you say you believe and to maintain the standards you have established for them.

It should come as no surprise that kids have a difficult time embracing a faith that we parents preach but refuse to practice. Further, we can't fool ourselves into believing that there isn't a direct connection between what we model for our kids and what they ultimately embrace as a way of life for themselves.

As parents we must never forget that our microphones are always hot. We simply can't have huge discrepancies between our Sunday suit and our Monday through Saturday lifestyle. Cheat anyone out of anything—be it something tangible or something intangible, such as taking credit for someone else's efforts—and don't be taken aback when your kids cheat in school. Let video games and Facebook run your life, and don't be surprised that they master your kids' lives too. Speak disrespectfully to each other or about someone else, and assume you'll hear the same attitude coming back at you.

Dad, make cheap or lewd comments about the professional cheerleaders who dance across the TV screen at halftime or, Mom, live for the next installment of TV's version of soft sexual fantasy shows, then don't be surprised when your teenage son or daughter goes looking for the wrong kind of love in the wrong kind of places. Our kids' behavior reflects the very things that the most influential people in their lives—Dad and Mom—value most.

Keep in mind too that not only can our disrespectful way of treating others backfire on us, but it can also sabotage our relationship with our kids. In fact, we parents can cause many of our children to wonder whether our spiritual values are even worth embracing.

Fortunately God, who is a Father Himself, laid a path for us when it comes to our children. He knew that we'd struggle as parents and that we'd sometimes get it wrong. That's why God put everything on the line on our behalf— and not because we deserved it. It was because it was our only hope. God reached out to people who have minds of their own and long lists of failures, and He rescued us. It's called grace! And without God's grace, we don't have a prayer for our parenting efforts.

GRACE-BASED PARENTING

Grace encompasses everything good about God's plan for humanity and is therefore the perfect context for raising our kids. We call it "grace-based parenting," and it is profoundly simple: treat your kids the way God treats His kids—with grace. Grace-based parenting is an others-oriented/others-first relationship strategy that encourages and equips dads and moms for their character profession.

*Grace encompasses everything good about
God's plan for humanity and is therefore
the perfect context for raising our kids.*

We'd like to share a practical and very effective way we ensured that our kids experienced grace in our home. It was grounded in our desire that our sons and daughters never suffered due to our shortcomings and mistakes: we gave them the freedom to be candid with us.[1] Our children must have the freedom to tell us what's weighing heavy on their hearts—even if it's something we've done that ticked them off or, in their opinion, an example of our not practicing what we preach. In the Kimmel home, both of us parents figured out early on that we were capable of doing things that irritated and hurt our children. We didn't want the root of bitterness to find its way into the soil of our children's souls (Hebrews 12:15). That's when we instituted "What's Your Beef?" nights.

WHAT'S YOUR BEEF?

The first part was simple. Each of the children could order anything they wanted off the Kimmel menu. If one wanted Chinese; another, Mexican; another, Italian; and the fourth, ribs, it was no problem thanks to the miracle of fast food.

The next part was harder but critical to the effectiveness of this night. We would let each child tell us anything we had said or done that embarrassed, disappointed, or hurt him. But here was the key: we couldn't defend or explain our words or actions. All we could do was sincerely say that we were sorry and ask for forgiveness.

It was often painful to hear things we'd done, either intentionally or unwittingly, that had caused our boys and girls hurt or sorrow. But it was a relief for all of us that these things didn't have to maintain their toxic position within our relationship. It's what people in a character profession do: we take responsibility for our actions and ask for forgiveness.

As our children got older, an interesting phenomenon evolved. They assumed they had the freedom to share what was on their hearts anytime they needed to. Our kids would occasionally pull us aside and say something like, "Dad/Mom, may I have a private 'What's Your Beef?' moment with you?" As we look back, we see those moments as gifts to our family's closeness and some of the most powerful opportunities we had to model God's grace to our kids. (By the way, as time went on, we needed to have the meetings only three or four times a year.)

GETTING A SECOND CHANCE

We parents—who are, by definition, in a character profession—don't always get it right. But our God of grace is the God of the second chance, the clean slate, the new day. No matter how old our children are, we need to jump at that second chance to receive God's grace and then extend it to our children.

Here are a few encouragements to get you started on that second chance:

- Develop a fresh relationship with God. In Psalm 51:10, David prayed, "Create in me a pure heart, O God, and renew a steadfast spirit within me."

- Don't be passive. Take the initiative to clean the slate between you and your kids.
- If family forgiveness is an ongoing struggle, talk to someone and get help for your specific problem.
- Maintain an attitude of brokenness, forgiveness, and responsibility for your actions when it comes to your children.

Basically, it all comes down to parenting the way our heavenly Father parents us. With His guidance and blessing, we are to treat our kids the way God treats His: with grace.

1. Tim Kimmel, *Grace-Based Parenting* (Nashville: Thomas Nelson, 2004).

The founders and directors of Family Matters (FamilyMatters.net), Dr. Tim and Darcy Kimmel are honored to equip families with grace-based relationships for every age and stage of life. They are speakers and authors of numerous books, including Grace-Based Parenting, Why Christian Kids Rebel, *and* Extreme Grandparenting. *Their greatest earthly joy comes from their children, their children's spouses, and an ever-increasing number of grandchildren.*

2

A Child's Number-One Influence

Dr. Kevin Leman

One spring several years ago, Bill Cosby and I were in Oklahoma City together to share in a presentation about preventing violence. Before the program, I spent a half hour alone with Cosby backstage. After a while, our talk turned to the topic of the evening—the influence of families on today's youth.

Cosby, whose son had been violently murdered, wanted to know my thoughts about what is happening to families in our society. The answer we discussed backstage emerged time and again that evening in our interaction with the audience: parents—not drugs, not movies, not peer groups—are a child's number-one influence.

That conclusion came as no surprise to me. Although we complain about all the influences on a child's life, we parents *are* what make the difference. More than any aspect of today's culture, your words, your silence, your presence, your absence, your example—both good and bad—all matter more in the life of your child than you may ever realize.

NINE PARENTING MYTHS

There are, however, nine myths about parenting that are prevalent in our culture today and that can sabotage our best efforts. See how many you've bought in to—probably without even realizing they aren't true.

Myth No. 1: "It's not the quantity of time with my kids that matters; it's the quality."

"Great news!" a husband calls to his wife as he heads out the front door with his golf clubs slung over his shoulder. "The Smiths have agreed to videotape Clovis's piano recital while I'm on the course with the new client. I'll be back this evening to tuck Clovis in!"

Trust me: when nervous little Clovis looks into the audience before his recital and sees the reflecting glass of the video-camera lens instead of his father's caring eyes, it's not going to be much consolation. Dad doesn't realize that although *he* may have felt he was there, his absence felt like a huge black hole for Clovis. It was a screaming statement of noninterest and poor priorities.

Generally speaking, the more your child spends time with you, the more stability and less uncertainty there will be in his life. This doesn't mean you should make your child the center of the universe, but your regular physical and

emotional presence, even in small ways, makes a big difference. Quality time does not make up for quantity time.
If you believe that myth, then you're doing so to rationalize your own selfish behavior. For a child, the *quantity* of
time you spend together is part of what makes it a *quality*
experience.

Myth No. 2: "I'm a good parent if I make many sacrifices for my child."

I was on the phone with one seven-year-old's parents.
They'd given their son the world. Unfortunately, he was
relishing his role as a tyrannical little Julius Caesar. They'd
given him every opportunity on the face of the earth and
even prepared him for one or two beyond—space camp, for
example, when he was only four years old. They couldn't
understand why their son, rather than embracing the ambi-
tions of a future astronaut, was hatching into a little alien. In
school he didn't finish any work, and at home he was beginning to mouth off to Mom and Dad. As I talked with them, it
quickly became evident that the problem wasn't that they'd
been uninvolved in his life. Instead, they'd *overdone* it.

Fully half of the parents who've walked through my
counseling door have overparented—either because of
perfectionist expectations or simply because they've been
revolving around their child as if she were the center of the
family's universe.

When you overparent, you weaken your child's self-
image, often suffocating her to the point that she comes to
believe she can't do anything without your help. Some par-

ents think they're sacrificing when they overparent. What they're really doing, though, is hovering.

When you overparent, you weaken your child's self-image, suffocating her so that she comes to believe she can't do anything without your help.

Imagine a hovering boss with impossibly high standards. After a few months of working for him, you'd sink into your chair when his shadow crossed your shoulder. You'd dread new projects. A hovering boss's attitude says, "You'll fail without my constant supervision." The "sacrificing" perfectionist parent sends the same message.

Overdo it enough and you'll reinforce habits you don't want to instill in your child. After all, children are born thinking about *me, me, me.* It's your job as a parent to help them begin to consider others before themselves. You don't want to create habits that last into your child's graduate-school education or marriage.

Myth No. 3: "Children should be free to express themselves any way they want."

My wife, Sande, and I were in a restaurant with a woman we hadn't seen in years. She'd brought her two little boys with her, and they were cuter than cute—the kind you'd find in a breakfast-cereal commercial. But like stereotypical child stars, they were unmanageable. The four-year-old was clearly trained in torture techniques. He began digging his fingernails into my leg under the table. Perhaps it was my contorted face that caused Mommy to try to divert his attention. In response, he started hitting her. "Oh, that's boys for you!" the woman said as she tickled her son to make light of his behavior. *Lady*, I thought, *boys are different from girls. But boys and girls alike need discipline!*

All kids need lines drawn in the sand to know what is simply not acceptable. I'm all for nurturing kids' personalities and gifts, but boundaries have to be drawn. Kids draw strength, stability, and self-esteem from boundaries, because boundaries help define what is safe and what isn't. Whenever kids take the reins, families end up in a mess. Yes, when their parents finally set boundaries, kids who have been in control will be unhappy and then test them. But as I say in my book *Have a New Kid by Friday*, "An unhappy child is a healthy child."[1] If your kids have been in control, it's time to stand up and be a parent!

Myth No. 4: "My child deserves the things I didn't have growing up, the things most kids today have."

When our daughter Lauren decided to try out for the school softball team, we didn't jump in and drop hundreds of dollars on the latest equipment and lessons with a softball pro to get her through the tryouts. She used her older sister's mitt, and since there was already enough aluminum leaning against the dugout walls to build an entire house, we figured she didn't need to own a bat.

Lauren made the team. Soon after practices started, she opened a dinner conversation by saying, "Dad, I need to get spikes." Notice the wording: not "*May* I have spikes?" but "I *need* to get spikes." I did not buy the shoes. Why not? Because Lauren's argument was "Dad! *Everyone else* has them."

I didn't want my child to expect that when she joined the hobby-of-the-month club, I'd fully outfit her with the latest high-tech gear. Young kids change their interests more frequently than their underwear. If you meet her every desire, you're training her to believe that whenever she wants something, all she has to do is turn to Dad or Mom, and you'll get it for her. And just how well do you think that's going to work someday when your kid is out of the nest, earning entry-level pay at her first job, and has begun racking up bills on her first credit card because she still has to have the latest and the greatest?

The way you respond to the latest and the greatest stuff now will set a pattern for your child's life. Are you always going to go along with the crowd, even if it doesn't make sense? Does that mean you don't get your kids anything? No, I didn't say that. What's important is that you think through your decisions carefully and that you give in moderation.

Myth No. 5: "A full plate of activities is good for kids. Let them experience all they can."

Many kids' activity schedules rival an Olympic athlete's training routine. Some parents take pride in this overcommitment because they themselves are running so hard on the wheel and wearing their busyness like a gold medal.

Unfortunately, they end up pulling their kids along on that same crazily spinning wheel of activities.

We all want the best for our kids, and we want our kids to be successful. But what is success to you? And does your definition of success really represent the type of true success—that feeling of affirmation and fulfillment—that will carry a child for life? True success is built on self-worth, on feeling good about who you are. It has nothing to do with constantly running on that little wheel, on doing more and more things so you can feel accepted. A healthy sense of self-worth is based on strong, healthy relationships, especially with family members, and the sense of belonging those relationships offer.

As I often say, "Activities are not good for kids." What your kids need most are your love, your care, and the security of knowing where they belong. They need leisurely love, and that won't happen while you run from point A to point B. That's why I recommend only one activity per child per term. You can't have regular, meaningful conversation if your kids are always out of the house learning how to hit a hanging curveball. You'd be amazed at the things you discover about your kids when you have unscheduled free time together. Just try it and see.

Myth No. 6: "A gifted child is a successful child."
Why is it that we parents have such a driving need for our kids to be number one? I talk with a lot of parents as I travel and speak around the country. And at least once on each trip I take, a parent will walk up to me after my talk, intro-

duce him– or herself, and then make this familiar statement: "My child is gifted." The parent's tone seems to imply that heaven is focusing all its attention on this truly extraordinary soul, and the rest of the world should get out of the way and pay homage.

Most people believe that a successful person is someone who has risen to the top and contributes to society. And what child is better positioned for this ascent than a gifted one? The truth is that we're all on a horizontal axis together; not one of us is better than the next person. We need one another because we're journeying through life together. That's what being a family is all about.

But here's what most people miss. Gifts are tools, and they're only as good as the one who wields them. Your son may be able to recite the value of pi to the tenth digit, but how fairly does he divide his candy with his siblings? Your daughter may be a cheerleader, homecoming queen, and valedictorian, but how well does she treat the "anonymous" girls who walk invisibly down the halls at school?

Intellect is a wonderful thing, but being smart can get your child into jail as easily as it can get him or her into MIT. Being gifted without having a healthy life attitude is like a Formula One race car without much rubber left on the tires—fast on the straightaways but dangerous on the turns. Life is mostly about navigating those turns, some of them hairpin sharp. Whether or not your child is "gifted," you can prepare her for life by focusing on her attitude rather than her accomplishments.

Myth No. 7: "Starting kids early in school will give them an extra edge."

Is your child a "little bluebird"? Little bluebirds know their colors and can sing their way through the alphabet. They can count from one to ten in Spanish along with their favorite *Sesame Street* characters, and they flit from word to word in their favorite book. And if that little bluebird has a fall birthday, academically it may seem to make sense to have him or her start school a year early.

Please don't. If academics are the primary basis for starting your child early, you're probably doing him or her a disservice. Socially and emotionally, your child may not be ready. When faced with the choice of making a child the youngest or oldest kindergartener, I'll opt for the oldest nine times out of ten.

This decision won't always make a difference right away. It may not pay off until the curriculum changes significantly—in fourth grade, for example, when homework really ramps up or in middle school when a child's body starts changing. Not starting kids early in school can make a tremendously positive difference in their lives, especially for boys.

Myth No. 8: "In today's competitive world, it's important that a child finish first."

Most of us discover early on that we don't always finish first. In fact, one of the most important lessons a child can learn is how to finish *last*, how to experience and learn from failure time after time—because life is filled with it.

17

Unfortunately, many parents feel their primary responsibility is to test the limits of their child's ability, to see whether he or she might be the next Shaun White or Shawn Johnson. But it's much more important to prepare our kids to live with their limitations than to give them an expectation of unbroken success.

Game-winning grand slams are not what make us who we are. What makes us who we are is how we get back into the batter's box of life after we strike out. Not having our own way or not finishing atop the dog pile of life isn't the worst thing in the world. Those experiences can teach us humility—the kind of thing your kid may need someday when he's married and has to know how to put his spouse's feelings first.

> *What makes us who we are is how we get back into the batter's box of life after we strike out.*

Myth No. 9: "If children set their minds to it, they can do anything."

If you set your mind to it, you can accomplish a lot—that's true. But you *can't* do anything just because you set your mind to it. Sounds obvious, I know. Yet the principle is easy to miss, especially when it concerns your kid. No matter how hard your child tries, he or she will never be able to reach certain goals.

A good parent recognizes a child's limitations and doesn't push the child with unrealistic expectations. Great expectations can push children too hard and too fast to do what they can't accomplish at all. And then what do you think they'll feel like? A failure.

Average is not a bad word. Yet so many parents start pushing their children early in life to become "above average"—as if being above average early on guarantees that little Felix or Felicia will be above average throughout life. Not so. There will always be someone who outranks little Felix or Felicia.

Here's the reality: By the time most of us hit our twenties, a few of us will be above average, a few of us will be below average, and the vast majority of us will be smack-dab in the middle. But in the end, does it really matter all that much? Where would we be without grocery clerks, doctors, farmers, construction workers, and others? The world needs different people playing different roles. How boring it would be—and frustrating—if we were all trying to be the same and do the same jobs.

Human development isn't a race; it's not about who gets anywhere first! Character takes seasoning and therefore really isn't seen until we're adults. Besides, you miss so much if you get caught up in the "my child can do anything" game. So instead of comparing your kid to others, enjoy him. In the same way you cultivate a flower, plant the seed, wait awhile, keep your eyes focused on your child, enjoy the first little sprout, and then let yourself be enamored with the beauty of what ultimately comes out—twenty years down the road. In the long run, what your child can't do doesn't matter. Who your child is says everything.

1. Kevin Leman, *Have a New Kid by Friday: How to Change Your Child's Attitude, Behavior & Character in 5 Days* (Grand Rapids, MI: Baker Publishing Group, 2008).

Dr. Kevin Leman, New York Times *best-selling author of* Have a New Kid by Friday, *is an internationally known Christian psychologist, award-winning author, radio and television personality, and speaker. Dr. Leman has taught and entertained audiences worldwide with his wit and commonsense psychology. He lives in Tucson, Arizona, with his wife, Sande. They have five children and two grandchildren.*

3

"It Was Like He'd Never Existed"

Gary Thomas

I was in my early thirties, a young father of three small children. This particular day I was traveling to a speaking engagement, waiting to be picked up from the airport. Ernie, my ride, was at a very different point in his parenting life: he was an empty nester with adult children. Ernie had worked hard to support his family, and now in retirement he was putting his energies into building up the men's ministry at his church.

Ernie had chosen early retirement from one of the most stable and well-known companies in the United States. Until the late eighties, if you could land a job with this company, you pretty much figured you had a job for life. The company paid well, but it demanded a lot of its workers. Ernie explained why he had walked away from that.

"We gave our lives to the company," Ernie said. "They took care of us, but [management] expected us to organize our lives around our work. If we ever said no, even once, we'd be taken off the promotion track and kept in a vocational eddy for the rest of our careers. So we got to work early and stayed late."

One of Ernie's coworkers was a younger man in his late forties who had worked side by side with Ernie for years. One morning the man failed to arrive at work, and Ernie assumed he was sick—until his wife called at 8:30 AM with the shocking news that the man had died. His heart had stopped while he was eating breakfast.

"They chose his replacement that afternoon," Ernie said, "and the man was on the job early the next morning— less than twenty-four hours after his predecessor was pronounced dead. We spent about fifteen minutes giving the new guy a quick orientation, but he was familiar with what we were doing, so it didn't take much time. Everything ran incredibly smoothly."

Ernie paused, gazing out the windshield, before he went on. "None of the other coworkers went to the guy's funeral. They knew the guy but didn't know his family; they figured it didn't matter much. After he was buried, as far as the company was concerned, it was like he'd never existed. He gave his entire life to the company, coming in early and working late, but the company didn't miss a step—not a single step—when he died. It's terrible to say this, but in a way, the company was less inconvenienced by his death than if he had taken a two-week vacation."

After the speaking engagement, Ernie dropped me off at my hotel, but his words remained with me.

IRREPLACEABLE?

The next day I opened the front door of our home, walked into the house, heard the familiar cry, "Papa!" and soon felt three pairs of arms around my legs and waist. My wife, Lisa, joined us on a walk, and Graham, who was then just four years old, held my wife's hand and mine at the same time, proudly proclaiming, "Now the whole family is together!" He kissed Lisa's hand and then kissed mine.

Kelsey, then just two, got a big smile on her face when she looked back at me and called out, "Papa's home!"

We had to ask ourselves, "How much is a weekend away from the kids worth?"

Ernie's words, "It's like he'd never existed," echoed in my mind. Earlier that fall, I had traveled eight out of nine weekends on behalf of a nonprofit organization. In anticipation of the new demands, my boss had given some of the senior team a generous pay raise. My wife and I were very grateful for this, but we had to ask ourselves, "How much is a weekend away from the kids worth?" During the week, a long commute meant I left home before the kids were awake, and I might not return until just an hour or so before they were in bed. Adding weekend travel to that weekday schedule was starting to look too expensive—even at an increased salary.

It wasn't easy to consider alternative employment—as an English major I'm not particularly marketable, business-wise—and since I had three kids at home and was committed to having my wife be there for them, the entire financial burden fell to me. But I also knew that if I dropped dead of a stress-related stroke, some nice words might be written about me in the organization's newsletter, and a few people would say, "Did you hear about Gary?" at the next annual conference, but sooner rather than later a capable replacement would be found, and the organization would do just fine. In the eyes of that organization—and I'm not faulting them—within a year, if not less, it would be as if I had never existed.

But the little feet that ran toward the door to greet me with the celebration and energy of a Macy's Thanksgiving Day Parade spoke an entirely different story. To my children, I was not replaceable. To them, my presence mattered enormously.

A LONG JOURNEY

After long conversations with my wife, and another year and a half of working as feverishly as I could on weekends and evenings to make it possible, I began a season of self-employment. I couldn't just get up and leave my previous job—making a rash decision is a luxury a sole wage earner can't afford—but I was determined to gain some kind of control over my schedule so I could choose who to disappoint with my absence. And I intended to place my wife and kids at the very bottom of that list.

I don't want to paint an overly optimistic picture or pretend that there weren't real sacrifices and risks involved. Our income went down the first year I worked at home. By the second year, things got so tight that one accountant told us we could declare bankruptcy. We didn't—but I doubled my efforts and we tripled our prayers. By the third year, we were actually earning more than I had in my last year of full-time employment. In the fourth year, our income rose considerably, and we could finally see on the horizon the possibility of being debt-free except for our mortgage.

> *The best payoff wasn't financial, but*
> *personal: I caught little moments*
> *throughout the day with my kids.*

The best payoff, however, wasn't financial, but personal: I caught little moments throughout the day with my kids, all of whom were homeschooled until high school. One day, when my youngest daughter was eight years old, she knocked on my office door and asked, "Do you have any balloons in your office?"

"No. Why would I keep balloons in my office?" I asked.

In a singsong voice, my little girl replied, "Because they're your favorite thing, silly. Except for eight-year-old girls, of course." With that, she was gone, never explaining the comment or the need, but blessing my day immeasurably.

I stayed self-employed for the next fifteen years until Kelsey graduated from high school. I'm back to working some very long days outside of the house, and once again have an employer. Yesterday, in fact, I arrived at the church at 6:30 AM, and I didn't leave until 8:00 PM. In the late afternoon, however, the same daughter who once asked me if I had any balloons in my office called to see if I would look over a paper she was writing for her college religion class. After we worked out the timing and caught up on each other's lives, she signed off with "I love you, Daddy."

She's nineteen now. She still says, "I love you, Daddy" just about every time she calls. That's worth a whole lot more than a paycheck. I can't imagine her—or my other two children or my wife—*ever* saying, "It's like he'd never existed." Thank you, Ernie. I don't know where you are now, but I owe you one. Big-time.

Gary Thomas (www.garythomas.com) is writer in residence and serves on the teaching team at Second Baptist Church, Houston. He is the author of numerous books, including Sacred Parenting *and* Devotions for Sacred Parenting. *Gary and his wife, Lisa, are the parents of three grown kids.*

4

Reassuring Your Kids of Your Love

Shaunti Feldhahn

Trust me: You get practical and insightful parenting advice when you listen to fifteen hundred kids! My own children were only three and six years old when I started doing research for a book that would uncover teens' common inner thoughts, fears, and needs that parents really need to understand.

As I interviewed and surveyed hundreds of tweens and teens for *For Parents Only: Getting Inside the Head of Your Kid*, I was sure their advice would also help me as my own kids grew. What nothing could have prepared me for, though, was the moment when one of my most sobering findings would come to life before my eyes, in the tearful words of my now eleven-year-old daughter. And it was basically my fault.

WELL-INTENTIONED ... BUT IT DIDN'T MATTER

My daughter is a sweet girl, but when she hit eleven years old, she began what I affectionately call "the eye-rolling phase." My husband, Jeff, and I were determined to nip it in the bud lest it become a habit. All well and good, right? So every time she spoke with a sarcastic tone, slammed a door for emphasis, or gave us *that look*, we sternly took her to task and made her repeat her actions or words more respectfully. Sometimes she did so willingly, but sometimes the situation deteriorated until angry words were spoken by both sides. As the months passed, I noticed that her normally kind, softhearted personality was becoming more volatile and less communicative.

It all came to a head one morning, not long ago, during the usual before-school rush. The night before, we had gotten in late from soccer practice. Since my daughter had elected—over my strong warnings—to spend the afternoon reading for fun instead of finishing her homework before soccer, I made her go to bed at 9:00 PM as usual, even though she protested that she wasn't sure she'd be able to complete her homework before school.

The next morning, with only fifteen minutes left until carpool, I saw her feverishly scribbling in her notebook, trying to complete her science assignment. I thought, *This is a good teachable moment to help her understand the consequences of her procrastination yesterday.* I walked over to where she was sitting and said in a sympathetic voice, "You weren't able to finish last night, were you?"

My sweet daughter looked up and snarled, "No, because you wouldn't let me!"

Well!

I felt that righteous-parent anger rise up, and I said, "Put your books away *now*."

I have always tried not to yell at my kids, but my tone was certainly cold with anger, and I saw her shrink down in her chair. "You may not speak to me like that, and you know it," I continued. "You chose not to do your homework when you had the chance, and you will have to tell the teacher that and take the consequences. Get in the van."

She rushed to obey me.

When her little brother and I climbed into the mini-van a few minutes later, I heard the sound of sobs from the backseat as I jabbed the key into the ignition. As I turned in my seat to back out of the garage, I looked toward her and said, "Why are you crying? You're the one who spoke to me rudely. You know that is wrong."

"I feel . . . *sob* . . . like I can never . . . *sob* . . . be good enough for you."

Instantly, my anger was replaced by terrible conviction—and concern. Here I was, forty-three years old, pouring out my anger on an eleven-year-old child. She certainly knew better than to be so disrespectful, but she's still just a child. She's still learning to control her words and actions. Yes, I can also have hurt, angry, or indignant feelings, but I have thirty-two more years of experience in controlling how those feelings are expressed—especially toward someone who I love more than my own life.

But that wasn't the only thing I realized in that moment. You see, because of my research, I suddenly knew what she *wasn't* saying but was privately feeling inside. She was not manipulating me or being a drama queen—the two most common suspicions of parents in such situations. Her reaction indicated something much more serious.

KIDS SECRETLY DOUBT THEIR PARENTS' LOVE

Over and over, as my coauthor, Lisa Rice, and I interviewed the teens for our book, it was clear that many of them truly, honestly felt that Mom and Dad were not always there for them when they made mistakes. That sounded benign at first, like an "oh, what a shame" sort of situation. But I soon realized this is the most dangerous perception children can have about their parents.

When the kids felt that they had received anger, discipline, or consequences *without* both a specific reassurance of love and the promise that the parent would walk through the consequences with them, some kids began to feel that their parents' love was conditional. In their minds, their parents' love seemed to go away whenever they made mistakes.

Hundreds of kids described for Lisa and me day-to-day examples of when (they thought) love was replaced by coldness, condemnation, or anger without explicit forgiveness and reassurance. A seventeen-year-old boy flouted a curfew and felt that he didn't lose just his driving privileges but the warmth of his parents too. When a fourteen-year-old girl spoke sarcastically and rolled her eyes, she felt that her mom's angry outburst wasn't just addressing her teenage failure to show respect. Her mom's reaction seemed to be saying she was a failure as a person. In those and hundreds of other examples, the teens felt that their parents were saying one thing: "I don't love you right now."

*Without both the specific reassurance of love
and the promise that the parent would walk
through the consequences with them, kids began
to feel that their parents' love was conditional.*

Early on, for example, a sixteen-year-old girl said this: "When your parents put your failures on a platter for you to see, it's hard because you already *know* you've failed. I think a parent needs to be there rather than trying to fix you. When I screw up, I know I need the consequences they give me, but I don't need to be fixed. I need reassurance. I need my mom or dad to listen and stand beside me rather than making it clear I'm not good enough for them."

Unlike most of the teens we talked to randomly, this girl's parents happened to be mutual friends with a couple we know well, so I knew they were a loving Christian couple who adored their daughter. I also knew this girl was reasonable and well-adjusted. Shocked and puzzled, since her words were teen code for "They don't care about me," I asked her, "What is it that they say or do that makes you think you're not good enough for them?"

Later, I asked the same question of the many other teens who made similar statements. The answers I heard were things like this:

- "It's when they get mad and stay mad awhile. It's scary when your mom or dad is furious at you. It's not about the punishment. It's that they aren't there during the punishment."
- "It feels like they will never forgive me. There's this unresolved displeasure just hanging out there. Like what I did is *so bad* that they're disgusted by my existence."
- "My mom doesn't come back around and say, 'We are disappointed, but we know people sometimes just make mistakes, and we forgive you.'"
- "They come down on me for the bad, but don't give me credit for the good."
- "They don't help me figure out how to handle it when I've screwed up. They leave me alone just when I most need them."
- "When I'm facing detention—again—they just shrug their shoulders like they don't care. It's like they're saying, 'We told you to be more careful. We're not getting involved. You have to figure this out on your own.'"

- "My dad doesn't talk to me when he's mad, but I never get grounded. It's horrible when I get the silent treatment."
- "They don't listen." (This is teen-speak for "They don't listen to how I *feel* about something.")
- "They freak out." (This is teen-speak for "They are showing visible emotion instead of being calm.")

Nearly all of the kids stated that, in the wake of their mistakes, they felt as if their parents' love had vanished and been replaced by anger, judgment, or condemnation. In other words, they felt that their parents didn't love them when they were bad, which raised the terrible (if subconscious) doubt about whether their parents really loved them at all. And in a small percentage of cases, teens were so thoroughly convinced that they were unloved that it was fatal for the parent-child relationship. Those teens completely and profoundly shut their moms or dads out of their hearts.

Lisa and I frequently compared notes about how tragic this entire trend was—tragic because it was so clear to us that it didn't need to happen. As parents (she had four teens), we could tell instantly that the examples the kids shared were *not* evidence of parents who didn't love their children, but of well-intentioned parents who were simply angry. Parents who didn't realize that their children needed not only correction and discipline in the face of mistakes, but explicit, ongoing reassurance of Mom and Dad's love as well. Parents who didn't realize how their kids would perceive their words and actions. Parents . . . like me.

KIDS NEED REASSURANCE

In shock, I just stared at my daughter. The words "I feel like I can never be good enough for you" hit me hard. I heard in my mind an echo of hundreds of other young voices, and I realized she truly was questioning whether her mom cared about her at all—and that she had been doing so for months.

I sent up a frantic prayer as I put the van in Park, unbuckled my seat belt, got out, walked around to her side of the van, and slid open the door. I leaned down and gave her a long, long hug. She didn't want to hug me back (one sure sign she had begun shutting away her heart without my realizing it), but I persisted.

"Honey, look at me." She wouldn't look up, so I spoke to her bowed head. "Honey, I'm so sorry. I had no idea I was making you feel like you're not good enough for me. Does that make you feel like I don't care about you?"

The little blond head nodded. "Of course it does."

"Honey, I'm so sorry. I love you and your brother more than my own life. It doesn't matter what you do wrong. Nothing could ever stop me from loving you."

A muffled sob. "It doesn't feel like that."

"I know, and I'm so sorry. I am so sorry if I have gotten angry at you without also telling you how much I love you. I am so sorry I've made you feel that I don't care about you. Can you please forgive me?"

She immediately nodded her head.

"Thank you, sweetheart." I hesitated, looked at the clock, and figured this was more important than the kids being on time for school. "Can you tell me what I do that makes you feel like I don't love you?"

Another little—and quavering—voice piped up: "It's when you get so angry at us."

My head snapped around. My eight-year-old son was looking at me from across the van, with tears in his eyes and his chin quivering in an effort to not cry. "I feel like that too."

Stunned, I looked back and forth between them and said, "Well . . . sometimes it's hard for a mom or dad to not get angry. Help me understand what feels so bad. Is the bad part that I *am* angry, or that you're in trouble, or that I'm punishing you, or that I'm speaking in an angry voice?"

"Speaking in an angry voice," they said in unison.

I asked the next question already knowing what I would hear: "Would it feel better if I were just as angry, but calm about it?"

When they both nodded, I promised them then and there that I would try my best. I asked them to tell me when I was getting my (in their words) "scary-angry voice." I promised I would ask God to help me love them like He loves all of us when we make mistakes. Especially, I promised to listen to my own voice and change my tone when I need to—something I have indeed had to do several times since then. Taking the advice of fifteen hundred kids, I have also (with God's supernatural help!) been purposeful about doing the *opposite* of the things I listed earlier. Instead I try the following:

- When I get mad, I try to show my kids that I'm not going to stay mad. I reach over, hug them, and say, "I'm angry, but I love you."
- Right away I say, "I forgive you."
- I say, "I'm disappointed, but it's just a mistake, and I know you'll do better next time."
- I try to notice their good choices and comment on them.
- When they get in trouble with me or others, I try to show them that I'm there for them—even if that means simply walking them into the school and saying, "I love you" when they nervously go to tell the teacher that they didn't complete their assignment on time.
- I listen for and acknowledge the roiling emotions under the surface of the problem ("Are you worried that you'll be embarrassed in front of your friends because you were grounded?").
- I try to stay visibly ultracalm when they are telling me something that they know Jeff and I aren't going to want to hear.

MAKING KIDS FEEL SAFE

In the months since that incident—and because I have become much more purposeful about exhibiting "calm anger" and *proving* my love in the face of their mistakes—I have seen my daughter emerge from her shell, share her feelings again, and risk telling me things she would otherwise have hidden from me. She has even returned to reaching out and taking my hand as we walk through a parking lot or the mall. My son is a bit too young for preteen rebellion, but he has become, if anything, even more affectionate than before. I have certainly messed up, but I have given my kids permission to tell me when I'm using that angry tone that scares them—and to their credit, they have tremulously done so. And they have cued me in advance as well: "Mom, can I tell you something without you getting upset?"

I learned many things and got some life-changing advice in my years of research with fifteen hundred teens, but certainly one of the most important is this: Kids don't look like it, but when they make mistakes they truly do wonder, deep down, if their parents really love them. And they need their parents to answer that question with a resounding yes.

Shaunti Feldhahn is a popular speaker, regular media guest, and the best-selling author of many groundbreaking research-based books, including For Parents Only *and* For Women Only. *She holds a master's degree in public policy from Harvard University, worked on Wall Street, and today uses her analytical experience to help people understand the most important truths about the most important people in their lives. She and her husband, Jeff, are active in their Atlanta-area church. They are the parents of two children. For more about Shaunti, visit www.shaunti.com.*

5

Know Your Kids!

Dannah Gresh

Bob and I weren't really ready to be parents. We were counting on five years of fun before we got really serious about the family thing. But God was in control, and in His wonderful wisdom, He gifted us with Robert William Gresh IV fifteen months after our wedding day.

Robby was every mom's dream baby. He never—I promise you—never cried! If his diaper needed to be changed or he was particularly hungry, he softly grunted. I kept working after he was born because caring for him at home was a bore. He was simply so easy, and he sat happily and quietly at our little marketing firm. So I kept writing marketing reports and enjoyed my new baby's coos and giggles.

Robby was always happy. In fact, one time Bob accidentally locked him in the car for a couple of hours—with all of us outside frantically trying to get it open—and he just smiled and enjoyed the wait!

So, you can understand my consternation when Alexis Ellyse Gresh entered the scene. What a day of surprises . . . First of all, the doctor had been so certain she was a boy. I felt so blessed when he told me we'd need to find a different name because I was having a girl. But then . . . they left me alone with that little bundle of girl, and something odd happened. That tiny bundle began to scream at the top of her little newborn lungs. Veins started popping out on her forehead and neck.

Something was very wrong! I pressed that wonderful red button to call a nurse as fast as possible—and I let the baby lie on the bed just in case touching her would complicate whatever was happening.

"She just wants to be changed," said a seasoned nurse upon a brief investigation.

"But she's . . . crying," I said. "Are you sure there's not something wrong?"

"They do that a lot," she said.

"Cry?" I asked.

"Yes," the nurse said. "This one is a little more vocal than some, but then again, you've been ignoring her." She picked up my daughter, changed her, and tucked her back into her acrylic hospital crib. Little Lexi was now quiet and happy.

My marketing career ended soon after baby number two's birth. Lexi was a full-time job. Thankfully she was more full of giggles, exploring, and fun than screaming and tears.

EACH CHILD IS UNIQUE

Children are as different from each other as night is from day. Since no two are quite alike, no two can be parented in quite the same way. That's why my best advice for any parent I meet is Proverbs 22:6, which reads: "Train up a child in the way he should go, even when he is old he will not depart from it" (NASB). I can't even remember who gave me this advice, but that dear individual opened up this single Bible verse to me in a way no one else ever had.

Since no two children are quite alike, no two can be parented in quite the same way.

Of course, the Bible outlines some specifics in the way we should parent. We should teach our children not to lie (Proverbs 6:16-17). They should study hard as students (2 Timothy 2:15). It's best if they learn to pray (1 Thessalonians 5:17). There is a lot of specific advice about the way we should raise our children, and in Proverbs 22:6 God affirms our choice to train our children according to these instructions from Him. In the original Hebrew, the word *train* is *hanak* and is best translated as "dedicate," indicating that our children are to be dedicated to God and His ways.

But there's something more that we can't miss here: The Hebrew word used for *way* in this verse is *derek*. Literally, it means "my way" or "bent." It was a Hebrew marksman's term—and by *marksman*, I mean the guy with the bow and arrow.

Back in that day, marksmen did not receive a standard issue bow and arrow with wires and buttons that would adjust the bow to their liking. (Even I could hit the broad side of a barn with a modern bow and arrow!) In Old Testament times, every marksman went out and found his own piece of wood and carefully crafted it into a bow. Since different kinds of wood have varying strengths and levels of moisture, the marksman probably spent many hours over many days to learn the unique "bent" or tendency of the wood so that he would be able to shoot accurately with the bow he crafted. The word *derek* refers to the process of learning about the wood.

This blew my mind! I suddenly understood why Robby and Lexi were so drastically different from each other and why parenting each of them had to be approached in a unique and custom-designed way.

It was as if God lit a spark within me, and I knew He was saying to me, "I have a specific way I'd like you to dedicate each child to follow, but to be successful, you've got to know the unique strengths and qualities of each one. Since that'll take some time, plan on investing it. In fact, it's going to take *a lot* of time."

Quality time? A myth!

UNDERSTANDING YOUR CHILD'S UNIQUE BENT

My kids demand that I study them. Well, it's not really their demand; it's God's. He wants me to know the kids He has entrusted to my care. We have to be students of our children—learning each child's "bent"—so that we can impart God's values in creative and personalized ways that will impact our children according to their unique differences.

If Robby were a piece of wood, he'd probably be a solid, thick piece of hardwood such as oak or maple; his personality reflects a deeply rooted strength. Today, as a young adult, he brings quiet stability and strength to each situation.

Lexi's wood would be curly willow. It's not a tall tree, but it spreads far and wide with playful branches. Lexi brings life and entertainment and energy everywhere she goes.

And we recently added Autumn Qiu Yun Gresh to the family. We adopted her when she was fourteen, and she's a winsome blend of our first two children. She's quieter than Lexi, but has a quick wit that pops up in the right setting. I see Autumn as a beautiful midsized birch with playful bark and breezy leaves that are easily swayed by the personalities around her.

We have to discipline, direct, encourage, call out, and coach each of our children according to who they are.

Each of your children and mine has unique strengths and unique weaknesses. And we have to discipline, direct, encourage, call out, and coach according to who they are.

Recently one of my kids was feeling insecure about our mother-child relationship because it looked different from my relationship with one of their siblings. To be specific, the child who approached me feared I was giving the sibling harsher consequences for bad behavior—and wondered why!

Thanks to the fact that Proverbs 22:6 has been a treasure to me, I knew exactly what to say. I explained: "I will never treat you or love you the way I do your sibling. You are not your sibling. You are you. And I will treat you and love you the way you were created and designed to be loved." Our conversation ended with a lot of openness and assurances that I loved them both equally but differently.

WHERE TO FIND QUANTITY TIME

Research supports my second best piece of advice, which is actually the anchor to my best piece of advice. It is this: Have family dinners more nights of the week than you don't. Family dinners don't happen much in most homes, and I think that's a big mistake. Having dinner as a family has been proven to increase academic success and reduce at-risk behavior.

A recent study showed that two of the activities most closely correlated with high SAT scores were eating family dinner together and being read aloud to as a child.[1] Both are simple ways to invest a great quantity of time in our children and be able to study and know them.

Meals not only create an opportunity to unravel the day's events and advise your kids, but they are also a springboard to more opportunities to spend time together as you discover what is on your children's hearts. For example, if Lexi heard that everyone is going to see a movie that sounds like a good one to see, we'll schedule family movie night for that weekend. If Robby's excited about paintballing, we'll go buy the stuff and prepare to die! If Autumn is missing food from her Asian heritage, we'll head to the Asian food store to buy chicken feet. If you aren't having family dinners, try it and see how it works.

Dinner is the anchor of quantity time. I protect it at any cost—and our family has five busy schedules to line up. Sometimes dinner happens at 8:30. Sometimes it happens on the go at Chick-fil-A, our favorite fast-food stop. But a family dinner almost always happens if we are in town. Why? Because I cannot study my children unless I am with them!

Tonight, I'm taking a stab at baked potato soup. Bob and I both know how it will go before it even happens. (We've been studying these kids for a long time now.) Robby won't say much, but he will enjoy it no matter how it turns out. Lexi will commentate, telling us exactly what she thinks of my new recipe—fantastic or failure. Autumn will humorously support them both.

And we'll all know one another just a little better at the end of the meal.

1. Edward M. Hallowell, *The Childhood Roots of Adult Happiness: Five Steps to Help Kids Create and Sustain Lifelong Joy* (New York: Ballentine Books, 2003), 174.

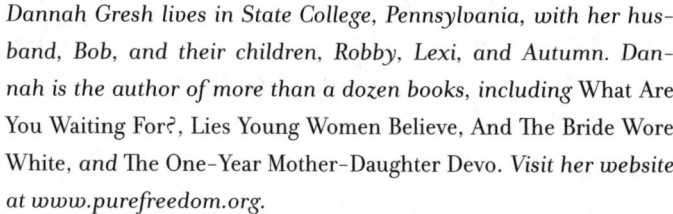

Dannah Gresh lives in State College, Pennsylvania, with her husband, Bob, and their children, Robby, Lexi, and Autumn. Dannah is the author of more than a dozen books, including What Are You Waiting For?, Lies Young Women Believe, And The Bride Wore White, *and* The One-Year Mother-Daughter Devo. *Visit her website at www.purefreedom.org.*

6

Talking to Your Kids About Sex

Ted Cunningham

I grew up in an independent, fundamentalist, premillennial, King-James-only church. Sex was a taboo subject. When it was discussed, all the advice we heard was "Don't," "Wait," and "Stop it."

The people in my church and home loved Jesus and taught me about Him. My parents read me the Scriptures, and we listened as my pastor preached the Word every Sunday morning, Sunday night, and Wednesday night. We learned that sex outside of marriage was sin. In fact, the words *sex, sin,* and *marriage* were often used in the same sentence.

Sex quickly became a bad word. Yet most of my friends in the church youth group succumbed to the evil and started sleeping around. Despite the purity rings, virginity pledges, and "Jesus, I'm sorry" prayers, they still had sex. As for me,

I grew up with great confusion about my body, sex, and the opposite sex.

Once married, I struggled to develop a healthy, fulfilling, and godly sexual relationship with my wife. Why? I had not been taught about sex or sexuality in a loving Christian context.

I am not alone. Since neither my church or my home gave me the advice I needed about sex, I am determined to break that cycle in my family and hopefully in yours too. After years of studying the Bible, searching for wise counsel, and working through my own problems, I've gathered lots of advice, and I've compiled some of it here.

WHERE DO WE START?

At every marriage seminar I teach, I reserve the final session for a candid conversation about sex. When the session ends, I usually hear questions like these: "How do we talk to our kids about sex?" "Where do we start?" "How far do we go?" Parents know sex education is a major part of growing up and preparing our children for life's milestones, but many moms and dads were never given proper information themselves and may not know where to start. I want to encourage you to start early, be clear, be candid, be open to questions, and don't ever stop talking to your kids about sex.

In an attempt to protect a child's virginity, some parents fall into the trap of using shame-based sex education. They use code words, minimal details, and shyness to address the issue of sex. This sort of education often results in a belief that sex is unmentionable or even dirty. It also leads to guilt-prone married sex.

GOD CREATED SEX

I am sick and tired of Christian parents feeling they are on Satan's turf when they discuss sex. This is not his turf; this is God's turf! God is holy. God created sex. He designed sex. He wants you to enjoy it. As a pastor, I am deeply concerned about the sex life of each member of our church. I want every church member to have great sex in God's intended context. And I want each child to know that what God created in sex is fantastic!

I have three goals for every parent in our congregation:

1. Start reading. Discover truths about sex, sexuality, and sexual intimacy straight from Scripture.
2. Start talking. The "sex talk" commonly known as "the birds and the bees" is dead—and good riddance! With the Internet, social media, and mobile devices preaching much about sex that is counter to our values, we need a long conversation that starts in preschool and continues through to marriage. Our culture exposes our children to innuendo and images at a far earlier age than we would like, so we need to start talking with them about God's design for sex early.
3. Stop the silence. We must reclaim sex as a topic to be discussed by churches and parents, not Hollywood

and schools. Be the first to write messages about sex and sexuality on your child's heart. Beat the world to the punch.

*Be the first to write messages about sex
and sexuality on your child's heart.
Beat the world to the punch.*

WE HAVE TO BE HONEST
AND START EARLY

My wife, Amy, and I are Corynn's parents. God gave us— but primarily my wife, since she's the same-sex parent—the responsibility to boldly proclaim His truths about her body, sex, and sexuality. We made the decision early on to tackle issues and questions head-on. Guarding our children's hearts means speaking with plain-and-simple honesty. That's why, when our kids ask questions about their body or sex, we say it like it is. Here's how to do so at different ages.

Birth to five years old
The best way to approach kids about the subject of sex is with prayer, grace, love, and honesty. All too often parents fall into the unhealthy pattern of using code words, a practice usually started when kids are young.

During preschool, a child's brain is developing rapidly. If you teach young children that their bodies are shameful things—and you can do that in subtle ways—then they'll believe that for years to come. That's why it's so important to avoid code names and to be totally honest with your children.

I will never forget the night my three-year-old son popped up out of the bathtub, looked at his penis, and asked, "What *is* this?" Depending on the parent, there is more than one answer to that question.

Many parents might say, "That is your wa-wa," or some other babyish code name. Wanting to be open and honest, I boldly proclaimed, "That is your penis, Carson." I vaguely remember using a deep voice as well. Wouldn't you know it? That became Carson's new favorite word.

That next Sunday, between services at Woodland Hills, I went over to our children's department to check on my little guy. When I got to his class, the teacher was very stand-offish. She eventually got up the nerve to ask me, "Pastor, may I talk to you for a second?"

I said, "Sure. What's going on?"

She asked, "Is everything okay at home? Is everything good?"

I said, "Yeah, everything's great."

What I didn't realize was that Carson had been using his new favorite word all morning. Okay, I didn't say your kids won't embarrass you sometimes, but the trade-off is worth it.

Mom and Dad, whether it happens during a candid conversation prompted by a Cialis commercial or at a teachable moment during bath time, we get to impress messages about sex on the hearts of our children. What they learn from us—from our words and our actions—will sink deeply into our children's hearts. They will take those lessons with them for the rest of their lives.

Six to nine years old

Teach about modesty, sexuality, and appropriate and inappropriate touching.

Carson was at my parents' house the other day when a well-endowed woman came on the news. He told my parents that she was "showing her line." He was, of course, speaking of her cleavage.

My mom asked, "Is it wrong to show that line?"

"It's not modest," he said.

"What does it mean to be modest?" she asked, waiting in eager anticipation for his answer.

Carson said, "You are not to squeeze them together like that. They have to be spread apart."

My parents spent the rest of the day with stomach pains from laughing so hard.

One more thing. Remember that sometimes lessons have to be repeated or explained multiple times, but making sure your kids are comfortable talking with you about sex and modesty is one of the most important goals of a healthy sex education. As we're finding, Carson is quite comfortable sharing his opinions.

Ten to thirteen years old

Teach these tweens and young teens about their desires. You say the same thing about their desires that you said about their bodies: "God created your desires. They are not dirty. We all have them. You are normal."

The single Shulamite woman may have been only a few years older than your kids are now when she experienced intense sexual desire for Solomon. She desired the love of a shepherd-king. Her desire and passion spilled over in one of the most graphic texts in your Bible:

> Let him kiss me with the kisses of his mouth—
>   for your love is more delightful than wine.
> Pleasing is the fragrance of your perfumes;
>   your name is like perfume poured out.
> No wonder the maidens love you!
> Take me away with you—let us hurry!
>   Let the king bring me into his chambers.
> (Song of Songs 1:2–4)

Don't freak out when your son or daughter begins to desire the opposite sex. Be sure to talk through the difference between selfish lust and healthy sexual attraction, which should only culminate in a loving marriage. And be open about your own feelings at their age. Don't lock them in their bedroom or send them into hiding. The more you freak out, the more you drive them to secrecy. It is critically important to keep the lines of communication open at this stage. This may not be on your list of favorite jobs, but the topics of masturbation, wet dreams, erections, pubic hair, fondling, kissing, petting, oral sex, pornography, and intercourse need to be addressed earlier rather than later. Kids will wonder about these issues and need guidance from you as their parent.

Fourteen years old and up

Teach your kids to honor marriage, not just purity. Get them ready for marriage. This idea is foreign to most parents in church today because it seems too early, but go with me for a second here. You prepare your kids for college and for what it takes to get a job and make money. That is obvious. But picture your kids getting married and having children. Do you want to see your grandchildren during the holidays? Then prepare your kids for a great marriage.

Marriage and sex—in that order—are wonderful gifts from the Lord. Our children should be prepared for both. And since your silence could lead to shame, guilt, paranoia, perversion, or premarital sex, speak up. Honoring marriage and talking candidly about sex will lead to healthy discussions and stronger families.

Ted Cunningham is the founding pastor of Woodland Hills Family Church in Branson, Missouri. He is the author of Trophy Child *and* Young and In Love *and is the coauthor of four books with Dr. Gary Smalley. Ted speaks each month with Gary Smalley at his national Love and Laughter marriage conferences. Ted and his wife, Amy, live in Branson with their children, Corynn and Carson.*

7

Setting Up Your Child to Succeed

Amy and Michael Smalley

Has your child ever been caught in an utterly ridiculous lie? You catch him with his hand in the cookie jar, but he looks at you and says, "What? No, I'm not sneaking any cookies." Our son Cole was only six years old when we caught him in such a lie, and we were surprised by how outlandishly confident he could sound telling his lie. That experience taught us a powerful lesson, and we believe it will help you as well.

I (Amy) had bought Cole a shirt during one of our seminars in a city somewhere in America (we travel so much it's hard to remember where). It was not necessarily an expensive shirt, but I had taken time to find it for him and picked out one that I thought he would like. After wearing it to school, Cole came home with a dramatically changed shirt. Hanging on my son's tiny six-year-old body was the remnant of the recently brand-new T-shirt. He had clearly taken some scissors and made hundreds of tiny vertical cuts around the now-destroyed bottom of his shirt. I think he was going after his own version of "slightly worn" or "fringe look."

As he neared the bottom of the stairs, I was horrified to see his shirt. I reacted instantly and asked him why he had destroyed his new shirt. Without hesitation, he looked at me and said, "I didn't do it on purpose. It was an accident."

An accident? Yeah, right. "Cole!" I said harshly, and I could immediately see him getting that glazed look on his face—a look you might be familiar with, the one you see when your kid is going into shutdown mode. It was as if Cole had just entered a self-made nuclear bomb shelter. The only thing I could think to do was call for Michael. I needed him to verify for me that I was not insane and that Cole's shirt had been destroyed, not by accident, but by his own hands.

I (Michael) had actually been in the kitchen the whole time, watching Amy and Cole interact over whether the shirt had been accidentally or purposefully destroyed. (It was quite funny to watch!) Amy seemed so intent on getting Cole to admit that he'd cut up the shirt by himself and on purpose. It is so normal to get into these kinds of going-nowhere arguments with your kids, especially when they aren't behaving well.

I walked out of the kitchen and over to the stairs where Amy and Cole were standing. The first thing out of my mouth was—in an agitated voice—something like, "Now, Cole, we all know you did this, so just admit it or you'll regret it."

(It's always a great idea to browbeat your kid with a general, nonspecific threat.)

At this point things were definitely getting heated between the three of us. Cole responded to my empty threat: "Daaad, I promise! This was an accident! I fell down the hill outside."

I couldn't take it any longer. I officially exploded and yelled back, "Are you kidding me? You're trying to convince me that you fell down a hill and your shirt ended up with hundreds of perfectly cut strips by accident? Go to your room—now!" I may have also added, "And you're grounded for life until you tell us the truth!" I truly can't remember, but like any parent, I'm capable of saying the goofiest things when I lose my temper.

Thankfully, neither of us followed Cole up to his room right away. We both busied ourselves with other things so we could calm down, and that's when the Holy Spirit convicted us about how we had contributed to the problem. Should Cole have lied about the T-shirt? Of course not, but the Holy Spirit tends to focus us on our role in the situation and typically doesn't get involved in blame games. The Holy Spirit knows that the best chance our family has for successfully resolving a conflict is to make sure each of us understands how we contributed.

The Holy Spirit tends to focus on our role and typically doesn't get involved in blame games.

SETTING KIDS UP TO SUCCEED

As you probably realize, we as Cole's parents had not responded well to his obvious lie. No matter what our children do, particularly when they are doing something sinful, we need to maintain control. We do not help the situation by acting just as unhealthily as our kids do. But the main lesson we learned from the Holy Spirit—the lesson that has stuck with us ever since—is that we were escalating with Cole when he did something wrong.

Cole is the big avoider in our family. He hates conflict, and what we learned that day was that Cole, in order to avoid conflict, often lies so he won't get yelled at. Our eyes and spirits were opened to the realization of how our yelling actually encouraged Cole to lie. We were setting him up for failure rather than helping him succeed at being an honest child.

We fully understand that the lying was Cole's responsibility, but as his parents, our responsibility was to set him up to be able to make a good choice. We want to be helpful assistants to Cole, not hindrances. When we yell in response to his behavior, though, we make it harder for him to do the right thing.

ASKING FOR FORGIVENESS

After both of us realized the error of our ways, we went upstairs to talk to Cole. He was nervous when we first entered his bedroom. (He was probably still trying to figure out what it meant to be "grounded for life.") We sat on his bed and asked him a very important question: "Cole, have you been feeling like we yell at you a lot when you do something wrong?"

His reaction was precious. He looked down, away from our eyes, and began to cry. Then he said, "Yes. I don't like getting yelled at." We could tell that he was not trying to get out of trouble. The tears were more about how he felt when we yelled than about his being in trouble.

We both got down on our knees, on Cole's level, and told him that God had helped us understand that we'd been yelling at him too much. We asked him on the spot to forgive us, which, of course, he did with open arms.

Does this mean that Cole was not in trouble for lying? No. There had to be a consequence to his lying, no matter what we had learned and how wrongly we had responded. We were able to give Cole a healthy consequence, unlike being grounded for life, and we were able to do it the right way—without yelling. Cole's punishment was simple and logical: do some extra chores to pay for the shirt.

CALMER HEADS

Parents need to understand that we play a key role in modeling the kind of behavior we want to see in our children. We must also realize the importance of setting up our children to succeed in life and relationships. And we need to be open to the Holy Spirit's wisdom about how our behavior—whether it's yelling or some other overreaction—sets our kids up to fail. When calmer adult heads prevail, our children will only benefit.

If you have a kid who struggles with telling the truth, ask yourself this question: "What, if anything, am I doing that sets him up to lie?" And always ask yourself, "Is my reaction toward my child over the top?" When we can put the situation into perspective in the moment, we gain credibility: our kids start to believe that we will not blow up every time they do something wrong.

Is my reaction to my child over the top?

Whatever the parenting issue at hand, trust the Holy Spirit to guide you and give you the right words. As we parent Cole, our message needs to be: "We believe you can tell the truth and do the right thing. We are not giving up on you. Your punishment will fit the crime, and we know you'll do better next time."

When you do blow up, go to your child and ask forgiveness. Nothing is more powerful than a kid seeing his parents humble themselves and ask for forgiveness.

Helping Cole understand the importance of telling the truth gave us the opportunity to learn some important lessons about parenting. We learned to ask the Holy Spirit to help us see how we were encouraging misbehavior—and to help us stay calm in the moment. We were also reminded of the importance of humbling ourselves and asking forgiveness when we don't stay calm. Children do learn what they live, so may God enable us parents to model the kind of living He wants our children to do and to set them up to succeed.

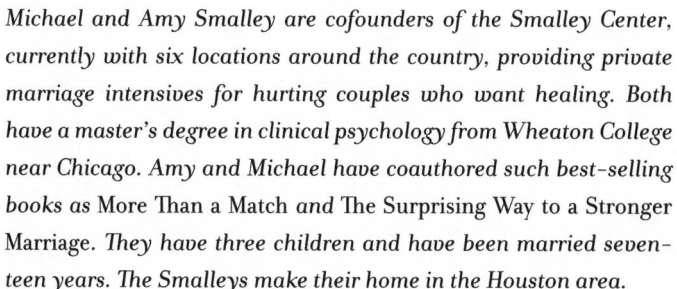

Michael and Amy Smalley are cofounders of the Smalley Center, currently with six locations around the country, providing private marriage intensives for hurting couples who want healing. Both have a master's degree in clinical psychology from Wheaton College near Chicago. Amy and Michael have coauthored such best-selling books as More Than a Match *and* The Surprising Way to a Stronger Marriage. *They have three children and have been married seventeen years. The Smalleys make their home in the Houston area.*

8

The Joys of Ditch Digging

Fern Nichols

As I look back over the many years I've been a mom, this is the best advice I ever received: anything of spiritual significance that happens in my children's lives will be because of God. He is the only One who can establish spiritual and eternal values in them. But there is a partnership—He chooses to involve me as a colaborer with Him. It was humbling for me to consider that God did not need my help, but in His sovereign plan, He invited me to take an active role.

When my four children were young, I read a book by Jean Fleming called *A Mother's Heart.* Chapter 5 of the book, called "God's Part, My Part," focuses on the first verse of Psalm 127: "Unless the LORD builds the house, its builders labor in vain. Unless the LORD watches over the city, the watchmen stand guard in vain." Listen to Fleming's wise words:

Knowing that God must work does not minimize our responsibilities. In Psalm 127:1, Solomon doesn't suggest that the builder neglect the building process, or that the watchman desert his post— but only that their efforts *alone* are not enough. The issue is faith, not desertion or neglect. . . . The mother recognizes that only God can make anything truly significant happen in her child's life.[1] [Emphasis added.]

A SENSE OF RESPONSIBILITY

Like most moms, I had a sense of great responsibility the first time I held each of my newborns. I wanted every one of them to love the Lord with all his or her heart, soul, and mind. I wanted them all to grow up to be responsible, God-fearing adults, and I took that divine charge quite seriously. And the content of Jean Fleming's chapter 5 helped me gain a proper perspective of what exactly my part was to be.

Basically, Jean compared mothering to ditch digging. To explain the metaphor, she told the true story of three kingdoms uniting to fight a common enemy, and they found themselves in trouble (2 Kings 3). While chasing the enemy through the middle of the desert, the army ran out of water. The king summoned the prophet Elisha to ask God what the kingdoms should do, and the prophet said the Lord's instruction was "Dig ditches."

Dig ditches? What? Can't you hear the soldiers complaining, *We're warriors, not ditch diggers!*

This was unglamorous, sweaty, backbreaking, thankless work.

But God said, "Make this valley full of ditches. . . . You will see neither wind nor rain, yet this valley will be filled with water, and you, your cattle and your other animals will drink. This is an easy thing in the eyes of the LORD; he will also hand Moab over to you" (vv. 16–18).

So the soldiers dug . . . and the next morning they witnessed a miracle. The ditches in that dry valley were now filled with water.

A CHANGE OF ATTITUDE

A mom's work may seem a lot like ditch digging—unglamorous, mundane, and monotonous. We wash and fold clothes, wipe noses, go to the doctor, do grocery shopping, cook, scrub toilets, clean up spills, help with homework, drive to piano lessons and sports activities, and so much more. As I read about my role in Jean's book, her message profoundly affected how I viewed the daily ditch-digging duties. I saw that the way I handled the mundane things I did every day could serve as an opportunity for God to do a miracle in the lives of each person in my family. After all, Jesus used the natural realm as His platform to demonstrate the supernatural, and God wants me to do the same. God wants my life to be a platform where He can reveal Himself to others. No longer I but Christ, so that He might manifest His life through me, using my home as a showcase to point my loved ones and others to Jesus!

Wow, this new perspective was life transforming! I no longer saw my day-to-day living as a series of endless chores, duties, and drudgery, but as opportunities to reflect Jesus. I now saw that my calling as a mother wasn't keeping me from doing something for Jesus, but instead was actually allowing Jesus to do something through me: He could use me to reflect His light and His love as I serve, as I minister life to my family, every single day! Luke 16:10 says, "He who is faithful in what is least is faithful also in much" (NKJV). By being faithful in the mundane duties of daily life, I had a beautiful opportunity to be a reflection of Jesus to my family.

By being faithful in the mundane mothering duties of daily life, I had a beautiful opportunity to be a reflection of Jesus to my family.

How did this revelation impact my everyday ministering to my family? My attitude changed, so the way I went about my responsibilities as a mom changed. Many times I would pray Scripture into a situation. For example, when I made sandwiches, I'd pray Matthew 4:4, placing my child's name in the verse: "Father, I pray that *Travis* will 'not live on bread alone, but on every word that comes from the mouth of God.'" As I assembled each lunch, I would pray over the child whose bag I was filling at the moment. The job was no longer monotonous. Instead it was a sweet time to cast my cares for my children on the Lord. It was a time for me to lay before the Lord my burdens for each child. (Years later my kids told me that their friends thought their lunches were so awesome that they often wanted to buy them. Hmmm, must have been all that prayer!)

When it came to washing three to five loads of laundry a day, I had to choose not to let the drudgery affect my attitude. So I began thanking the Lord that I was physically able to do the wash. I would think of a Scripture to pray as I washed and folded the clothes. One I often chose was Colossians 3:12: "Gracious Lord, I pray for *Trisha* that you would clothe her with 'compassion, kindness, humility, gentleness and patience.'"

One day my husband, Rle, surprised me with this affirming note: "Thanks for your loving care, which is so faithfully shown through the endless washing and ironing. [Yep, I ironed back then!] Each of us, especially our children, always go about the day knowing they are deeply loved because of your consistency in these areas." Now don't let this note make you think I was perfect. At times I definitely did not reflect the image of Christ in my role as a mother, and then I needed to ask forgiveness of my children as well as confess and repent before the Lord.

SETTING PRIORITIES

In order to see my role as God saw it, I purposed to make Him my number-one priority. I knew that I constantly needed to keep before me His great example of how He served others. That only happened when I intentionally set aside time to read the Word and pray. We human beings truly do become like the one—or the One—we spend the most time with.

My family was my number-two priority, but oftentimes other "important" things would creep into that position. Even though I served as president of an international ministry, I was determined to keep my children and husband a priority over Moms in Prayer. (In early 2012 Moms in Touch International, or MITI, changed its name.) When the kids got home from school, I changed hats and was fully mom. No more answering phone calls or doing ministry work. My focus turned to them.

What a privilege to colabor with God for the lives of my children! How wonderful that by His sovereign choice, He invites me to take part in His work in their lives. Jean Fleming summed it up so well:

> As mothers we can do nothing to persuade or convince our children to love God. We can dig the ditches, but we can't fill them. We can teach our children about God, pray for them, live the Christian life before them, and expose them to others who love and serve God. But only God can give them spiritual life.[2]

THE PRIVILEGE OF PRAYER

And that is why I pray. Prayer is truly the greatest work I can do on behalf of my children. When I pray, God hears and answers. Prayer releases His almighty right hand to do miracles in their lives. When I pray Holy Spirit-directed prayers according to His Word, that time with the Lord brings peace to my soul and turns my fears to faith.

When I pray Holy Spirit-directed prayers according to His Word, that time with the Lord brings peace to my soul and turns my fears to faith.

There was a time when my teenage son was hanging out with people who didn't love God and were making bad decisions. I dug into God's Word and prayed 1 Corinthians 15:33–34: *Heavenly Father, I pray that my son would not be deceived: "bad company corrupts good character." May he "come to back to [his] senses . . . and stop sinning."* The struggle lasted for some years, but one divine moment happened when he came back to God. He is now married to a woman who loves Jesus with all her heart, and they are raising their son to be a Jesus-lover.

There is always hope for our children when our hope is in the Lord. That's why the best advice I can share with you as a parent is to completely depend on God as you "dig the ditches" of service, of training your children in His way, and of prayer. I find it very comforting as a mom—and now a grandmom—to know that my ditch digging is important work, eternal work. How grateful I am that I can fully count on my God to fill the ditches with life-giving water. And He'll do the same for you.

1. Jean Fleming, *A Mother's Heart: A Look at Values, Vision, and Character for the Christian Mother* (Colorado Springs, CO: NavPress, 1982), 73.

2. Ibid., 74.

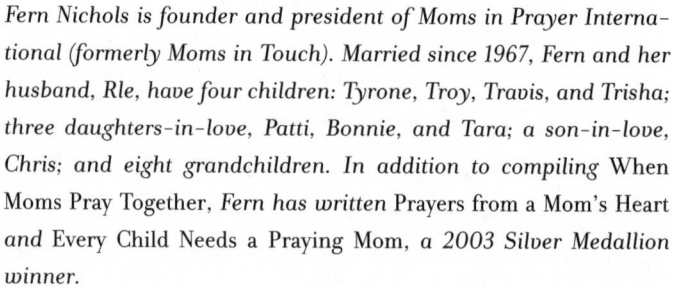

Fern Nichols is founder and president of Moms in Prayer International (formerly Moms in Touch). Married since 1967, Fern and her husband, Rle, have four children: Tyrone, Troy, Travis, and Trisha; three daughters-in-love, Patti, Bonnie, and Tara; a son-in-love, Chris; and eight grandchildren. In addition to compiling When Moms Pray Together, *Fern has written* Prayers from a Mom's Heart *and* Every Child Needs a Praying Mom, *a 2003 Silver Medallion winner.*

9

Joy That Money Can't Buy

Randy Alcorn

Through the years, my wife, Nanci, and I received good parenting advice from many people. But here I want to share what our all-wise Counselor named God taught us. The lessons came as He guided our family on a path that we would never have chosen without His leading. The bottom line of what He taught us is this: Nanci and I knew it was not good to sacrifice our children *for* God's kingdom, but we learned it is good to make sacrifices for His kingdom *with* our children. We were able to walk that path only because of God's grace and a lesson He had already taught us: everything—including our children—belongs to God.

ON THE INSIDE OF WHAT GOD IS DOING

In 1977, two years before our first daughter was born, I became the pastor of a new church. I also served on the board of the first crisis pregnancy center in the Northwest, and Nanci and I opened our home to a pregnant teenager, helped her place her baby for adoption, and saw her come to faith in Christ. By 1989, I was making a good salary as a pastor and earning royalties from writing.

Then something happened that turned our lives upside down.

Due to my concern for unborn children, I began participating in peaceful, nonviolent rescues at abortion clinics. I was arrested several times and went to jail. One time an abortion clinic won a court judgment against me and twenty others. I told the judge I would pay anything I owed, but I couldn't hand over money to people who would use it to kill babies. When I discovered that my church would receive a writ of garnishment, demanding they surrender one-fourth of my monthly wages to the abortion clinic, I resigned.

The only way I could keep my income away from the abortion clinic was to make no more than minimum wage. I'd already divested myself of all book royalties; our family lived on only a portion of my salary; and having just made our final house payment, we were out of debt.

The advice I sensed from God was this: Nanci and I needed our daughters' prayers and hearts to be with us. Ages eleven and nine at the time, Karina and Angela needed to be on the inside, not the outside, of what God was doing. Nanci and I decided to speak openly to our children about what was happening so they could pray and learn to trust God alongside us.

Sometimes we took the girls to abortion clinics so they could pray with us for the mothers who, deceived and heartsick, came to kill their children. To Karina and Angela it was clear: Jesus loves the little children, and if you love them too, you should stand up for them. We also taught our daughters that Jesus loves the mothers and that Christians should be the first to offer them every possible form of help.

We kept Karina and Angela informed and involved in what we were doing. They knew that their mother went down to the abortion clinic to talk with women every week, sharing the gospel and offering abortion alternatives.

CHOOSING TO STAY IN THE PRESSURE COOKER

In 1991, nine months after I resigned from the church, we were set for another major courtroom trial. It seemed almost certain we would lose this case, lose our house, and lose the ability to send our girls to the Christian school they loved.

Twelve hours before the trial, our attorney called. "Randy, I just received a fax from the abortion clinic. They want to drop you from the lawsuit."

Amazed, I felt immediate relief. The house was no longer in jeopardy. The girls could continue in school. We'd be saved the burden, tension, and glare of the media spotlight. But I was confused. "Why would they drop me?" I asked.

"You were a pastor, and you're an author. You've gotten a lot of press, and you've been explaining why you stand up for unborn children. Maybe they think that if they get you off the case, you won't have a platform to appeal to the jury or the public."

"Do I have a choice?" I asked.

"If they'd dropped you a few days ago, you wouldn't. But because it's within twenty-four hours of the case going to trial, the law requires that you agree. Obviously, you should!"

I told him I'd call him back, then I sat down with my wife and daughters. I explained what the lawyer had said and asked, "What do you think we should do?"

Karina, our eleven-year-old, replied, "Daddy, if the abortion people think they'll be better off without you, then I think God wants you there." Angela, our nine-year-old, nodded her agreement.

I reminded them of the potential loss of our house and their school. It would probably affect our lifestyle and ability to take family vacations. They understood perfectly. As much as Nanci and I wanted to climb out of the pressure cooker, we fully agreed with our daughters. We prayed and sensed God's clear leading.

I called our lawyer back and shocked him: "We've decided to stay in the lawsuit."

What followed was a whole month in court, a whole month of false accusations. We realized something the jury didn't: people who kill children for a living won't hesitate to lie under oath. We appeared to be the bad guys while the clinic owners and physicians, getting rich by killing children, were seen as heroes, as selfless advocates of women.

Although the judge was openly hostile toward us, several amazing things happened at the abortion clinic while the trial was taking place. Three employees quit. One explained to a pro-life protester outside, "It's like I suddenly woke up and realized we're killing babies here." When we heard such reports, we always shared them with our daughters. This wasn't just Dad's thing or Mom's thing. We were all in it together.

When the judge gave his final instructions to the jury, he said, "You *must* find these people guilty and punish them sufficiently to ensure they'll never do this again." For our totally nonviolent actions, the jury awarded the clinic $8.2 million.

MORE IMPORTANT THAN MONEY AND THINGS

By all appearances our lives had taken a devastating turn. Yet what others intended for evil, God intended for good (Genesis 50:20). We started Eternal Perspective Ministries. Nanci worked for a secretary's salary, supplementing my minimum wage. All of our assets, including the house, were in her name only. I had access to them, but legally I owned nothing. Ironically, I'd written extensively about God owning everything in *Money, Possessions, and Eternity*, and now, within a year of its publication, I owned nothing! In the crucible of adversity, God was teaching me life-changing implications of the truth I'd written about.

We reminded our daughters that God owned everything. So why worry about whether we would keep the house? It belonged to God anyway! He could easily provide another place for us to live. The clinic never got our house, and an anonymous donor paid our children's school tuition. But even if we had lost it all, God would have been faithful. He just would have—faithfully—led us along a different path.

Don't get me wrong. We weren't martyrs or heroes. While our sacrifices are tiny compared to the sacrifices of countless others, God showed Himself faithful, and our children saw it. Karina and Angela witnessed the reality of spiritual warfare, the battle for the civil rights of precious human beings, and the faithfulness of our gracious God. The girls, not just their parents, had been willing to sacrifice in order to please Jesus, our Audience of One. After all, His opinion is the only one that ultimately matters.

Having made Eternal Perspective Ministries the owner of the books I wrote, our family received no royalties—but suddenly my books were on bestseller lists. I told the girls I thought God was selling the books not only to change lives but also to raise funds for ministries close to His heart. And that made perfect sense to them. Since starting EPM—and by God's grace—we've given $6 million toward missions, famine relief, Bible translation, and pro-life ministry.

Years later, when I was riding bikes with Angela, we stopped to admire a huge, beautiful new house that was for sale. I said, "You know, if we'd kept one year of royalties, we could pay cash for that house. Do you wish we'd done that?"

Knowing all the ministries we support and the people we feed with those royalties, she laughed and said, "Dad, it's just a house!"

Tears came to my eyes. I thanked God for what He had taught not only Nanci and me, but also our children. From a young age, our girls understood something so many adults don't: that there are things in life far more important than money and possessions.

From a young age, our girls understood something so many adults don't: that there are things in life far more important than money and possessions.

INVITE KIDS TO EXERCISE FAITH

Nanci, the girls, and I have never thought, *It's a big sacrifice to give away that money.* On the contrary, we've felt joy, and we've experienced the truth of Jesus' words: "It is more blessed [happy-making] to give than to receive" (Acts 20:35).

Nanci and I never sacrificed our children *for* God's kingdom work. Instead we invited them to exercise faith in Christ and sacrifice *with* us—never realizing what an inspiration they would be to us. Our girls wanted us as a family to "speak up for those who cannot speak for themselves" and to "defend the rights of the poor and needy" (Proverbs 31:8–9). We saw this evidenced in countless ways, including when, as a high-schooler, our daughter Karina went and stood in front of an abortion clinic to give a friend one final opportunity to change her mind and let her baby live.

How your family chooses to help the poor will be different from the way the Alcorn family has. After all, different families face different circumstances. But every Christian parent can ask God to guide their outreach to the needy, can speak up for the rights of others, and can include their children in making personal sacrifices for the cause of Christ. Maybe God will call your family to lower your standard of living and raise your standard of giving. Maybe He will lead you to open your home or go overseas to help the needy and share the gospel.

This much I feel certain of: Our daughters' decision regarding that lawsuit cemented their allegiance to Jesus. Our children joined us in making sacrifices as we followed Christ, and now, twenty years later, my daughters are married to godly men, raising our five grandchildren to follow Christ, and consistently loving God and their neighbors. By God's grace, Karina and Angela and their husbands are passing on to their children a Christ-centered, eternity-minded joy that money can't buy and adversity can't take away.

Randy Alcorn is a best-selling author of more than forty books. He is also the founder of Eternal Perspective Ministries (EPM), a nonprofit ministry dedicated to teaching principles of God's Word and assisting the church in ministering to unreached, unfed, unborn, uneducated, unreconciled, and unsupported people around the world. He and his wife, Nanci, live in Gresham, Oregon, and they have two married daughters and five grandchildren.

10

Garden-Variety Parenting

Phil and Heather Joel

I remember the moment Heather and I found out we were having a boy. We watched the computer screen in the ultrasound room with nervous excitement as we waited for the news to be revealed. We already had a beautiful little girl who was a joy in every way, and though we knew we'd be completely happy either way, we were secretly hoping for a little boy.

My mind raced as I imagined all the things we could do together when he was bigger . . . soccer, rugby, camping, fishing . . . and, of course, music. Yes, he would be my very own little drummer, and we could go out on the road together, just him and I. A dream come true!

Our thoughts were interrupted by the sonogram technician. "Well, get ready. You had it easy with your little girl—but here comes trouble!"

Trouble? I thought. It was a weird moment. I'd heard the nurse right, hadn't I? "Do you mean we're having a boy?" I asked. Excitedly, I brushed off her words of doom and embraced the wonderful news. Heather and I were ecstatic!

Over the next several months as we prepared our hearts and our home to receive our new little family member, we would frequently hear comments like "Oh man, get ready! Your life is going to change *big-time!*" or "You've got one of these coming?—*pointing to own child*—You aren't gonna know what hit you," or "You guys thought you had it made with a sweet little girl. Just you wait! You're about to get a run for your money."

Comments like these coupled with the classics like "Boys will be boys" and "He's going to be *all boy*" swirled around in our thoughts like a whirlwind. Was there some secret club that people were trying to prepare us for without actually telling us outright? Were our lives really going to change that much? Were boys all alike? Was God about to trick us by handing us a messy, rough, rude, hitting, back-talking, naughty, noncompliant creature who couldn't sit still so He could sit back with His arms folded and laugh as He watched us struggle to figure out what to do? Were we doomed?

Well, the big day came, and we welcomed our beautiful little boy into the world. He was amazing. Our hearts were full, and all seemed right with the world. *So far so good*, we thought. *He loves to eat, he's sleeping through the night, he laughs, he smiles, and he loves to be held.*

A NEW PATH

Well, suffice to say, new challenges and new behaviors began to emerge when our son was somewhere around a year and a half old. And thus began a new (and slightly grittier) chapter of parenting: Welcome to the Twos. Challenging? Yes. Confusing at times? Definitely. Tiring? Absolutely.

Yet, in the midst of it all, something occurred to us that set us on a totally new path. The Lord used a simple childhood memory to redirect our thoughts and get us in line with His thoughts. You see, Heather's mother is an amazing gardener. All throughout Heather's childhood and even now, Nonny—as we call her—filled their house with beautiful flowers from her backyard garden. Every morning she'd wake up early to water, weed, and tidy up. Her garden always looked clean and lovely. She inspired Heather and me to do the same.

Somewhere in our son's second year, the Lord brought gardening to the forefront of Heather's mind. She had had one of those parenting 9-1-1 moments and was feeling exhausted and out of strength. As she was literally crying out to the Lord for wisdom and strength for that specific situation, He brought to her mind the concept of gardening as a picture of parenting. Consider these two insights.

NO. 1: KNOW HOW AND WHEN TO WEED

First, like your life and mine, a garden is meant to be beautiful, green, and full of good fruit. Plants begin as seeds. In order to grow, they need good soil, lots of water, and sun. Parenting is very much like gardening. We are given little people who need to be nurtured. It is our job as parents to tend their little lives and help them to grow in the Lord. However, the enemy has other plans for them and will do all he can to make our job seem impossible and hopeless. He tries all he can to riddle our gardens with weeds.

Weeds show themselves in the form of a sinful nature that will try all it can to serve itself and to get whatever it wants in order to gratify itself. Weeds can grow when the garden is either unattended for periods of time or exposed to unwanted seeds. Practically speaking, weeds can grow when we allow wrong behaviors and attitudes to grow in our kids and thrive unnoticed. Weeds will grow when we feed on a culture filled with junk that most people call "normal."

Proverbs 22:5–6 says: "Thorns and snares [and weeds!] are in the way of the perverse; he who guards his soul will be far from them. Train up a child in the way he should go, and when he is old he will not depart from it" (NKJV). Good gardeners knows that it is their job to cultivate the good stuff and weed out the bad stuff. Gardening takes great care. For example, a weed that is quickly snapped at the surface may appear to be gone forever, but if the root remains, it's only a matter of a day or two before the weed pops back out of the soil and continues to grow and gain strength.

The only way to truly remove a weed is to carefully dig out the underground root—and that kind of gardening takes *time*. If weeding is done when the plant is tiny, it can be pulled out with relative ease, roots and all. If neglected, however, the root of that weed will grow stronger by the day and eventually prove to be a major issue. This same principle—and the best piece of parenting wisdom we ever received—applies to the garden of our children's hearts too: If we ignore the weeds or take a quick approach to getting rid of them, they'll soon pop back up, more entrenched than before.

The only way to truly remove a weed is to carefully dig out the underground root.

Making time for the garden

One of the major issues Heather and I have wrestled with as parents is "Do we have the time to do this job well?" Are we slowing down enough to, first, even see the weeds and then to carefully pull them at the root? If not, what things in our lives need to go? What activities and concerns are taking away the time we need to do this parenting thing really right?

As we asked ourselves these questions, the Lord began to show us changes that we, as parents, needed to make. He showed us how to slow down, and He gave us new strategies to employ, things we could never have seen on our own. Slowly but surely we began to see beautiful things grow in Eden's little heart. As we saw real, tangible change, we became more and more excited and motivated to become even better, even more focused gardeners.

We live in a world that is in total opposition to godliness. Our culture is not at all on our side in our efforts to raise children who know and love the Lord. Rather than offering any support at all, the world we are raising our kids in offers a slew of the latest techniques, tips, ideas, and medications that promise to help us get through the job we've been "stuck with."

The world would have us believe that a normal little boy is a rude, hyperactive, noncompliant, disobedient little punk. And *diva* has become the latest height our little girls are supposed to aspire to. (Diva? Really? Doesn't that stand in sharp contrast to the fruitful, others-centered, thriving Proverbs 31 women we are called to raise?) Knowing what God has to say about parenting, I just can't roll with those kinds of messages. After all, I've never read in the Bible about these caveman-esque characteristics being ingrained into the male race. Rather, God refers to godly men as strong leaders, worshiping warriors, and lovers of their wives and children. The Lord teaches that the greatest leaders are the greatest servants and that the men who passionately seek Him will have homes filled with peace.

NO. 2: IT'S ALSO ABOUT ENJOYING OUR KIDS

The cool thing about gardening is that it's not just about keeping away the weeds. Gardening is really and truly about getting to enjoy the fruit of our efforts. God doesn't want us merely to survive our parenting, but to actively teach and train and shape our children's hearts so we can enjoy them right now and as they continue to grow. Such enjoyment marks the difference between just surviving and really thriving!

God doesn't want us merely to survive our parenting, but to actively teach and train and shape our children's hearts so we can enjoy them right now and as they continue to grow.

The Gardener of Our Hearts

In addition to being a great picture of parenting, the gardening metaphor also offers us an important truth for our own lives as parents. The Gardener of our hearts is the Lord, and He calls us to be alert to the ways the world wants to hinder our walk with Him. To keep our own lives clean and free of weeds in this crazy world, we need to spend time with God every day, feeding on the truth of His Word so we can continue to grow and bear good fruit as parents.

If we want to be the parents the Lord desires us to be— if we want to train our children well as He exhorts us to do in Deuteronomy 6:5–9—we must be totally dependent on Him and desperate to hear from Him . . . every day. After all, each day presents challenges, difficulties, and struggles. How can we expect to survive—much less thrive and grow— if we aren't personally seeking the Lord and growing in our own relationship with Him? It's through that primary relationship that He shows us His thoughts, ideas, and strategies not just for our parenting, but for every area of our lives. That starting point—each parent's relationship with the Lord—is key!

Psalm 128:1–3 talks about God's heart for family: "Blessed is every one who fears the Lord, who walks in His ways. . . . Your wife shall be like a fruitful vine in the very heart of your house, your children like olive plants all around your table" (NKJV). Clearly, God's vision for us—and for our kids—is to be *green, growing,* and *fruitful!* He would never give us a task like parenting that can't be done. That's not the God we serve. He always casts a clear vision and then gives us the tools to move toward it as we seek Him.

In 2004, Phil and Heather Joel founded the ministry Deliberate-People (www.deliberatepeople.com), an organization that helps people turn their passion for God into a plan to daily pursue Him through prayer and Bible reading. A New Zealander and musician, Phil has spent seventeen-plus years in contemporary Christian music. He has six solo albums. Phil and Heather grow their garden in Tennessee.

11

Our Godly Pediatrician's Best Advice

Gary Smalley

In 1976 I took a position as the marriage and family pastor at a large church in Waco, Texas. Growing up, I'd been a poor student. I couldn't type, I was dyslexic, and I had ADHD. I had struggled throughout my entire life preparing for my vocation, so I was thrilled to finally be gainfully employed as an assistant pastor.

While at that church, I developed a premarital Sunday school curriculum, put together a little seminar for engaged couples, and was doing a lot of counseling. God opened doors, and things were starting to happen in my ministry. I was feeling pretty good about that part of my life.

At home, though, things weren't going quite so well. Here I was, the marriage and family pastor, and our home life was a chaotic mess at times. Our kids were constantly fighting with one another and were very disrespectful to me and my wife, Norma. They refused to cooperate with us and were often out of control.

Norma and I tried everything we could think of—bribery, gifts, consequences. We even tried spanking, although we didn't feel good about that option. We weren't totally against spanking, but we just thought there had to be a better way. No matter what we tried, though, nothing was working.

One day I happened to be in our pediatrician's office. Dr. Charles Shellenberger was a leader in our church and a godly man whose family I admired. On this day I was particularly frustrated about the situation with our kids, so I told him what was going on and asked him how he would handle it. Dr. Shellenberger told me something that was simple yet profound. He said, "The key to healthy relationships is to keep honor high and anger low."

He went on to explain, "Here's what we did as a family that really worked for us. What you do is sit down with your children and ask them to help you organize your family so that everyone is highly honored and the level of anger will be as low as possible. There is a system you can use that does that." I was all ears.

"You will write a family constitution, like a family contract."

Our kids were quite young, and I said, "Whoa! That sounds great, but how do we do that?" And he explained further.

I had such trust in this man—the father of four older kids who were sharp, mature, responsible, loving, and actively following God. I was so impressed with them that I thought, *If his methods could produce kids like that, I would love to do half of what he has done so well as a dad.* I had such confidence in what Dr. Shellenberger said next that I couldn't wait to go home and share his suggestions with Norma.

CREATING A FAMILY CONSTITUTION

I rushed home and asked for a family meeting. We sat around the kitchen table, and I said, "Dr. Shellenberger has given me an idea. Let's try it and see if it helps us as a family." Everyone agreed. I addressed the kids: "Mom and Dad are really frustrated, and I'm sure you guys are too. You don't know when you're going to get spanked, you're uneasy, and you don't know what the rules are. There are no boundaries in our home."

We asked the kids, "What's it going to take to bring some harmony to our family?" They made various suggestions. One idea, for example, was "Let's pick up our stuff after we use it and put it away." And Norma quickly replied, "That'd be awesome! You know, I've felt like I'm the only one who cares about picking up the house." They all agreed that would be a good family rule, so we wrote it down.

Next they said, "Well, we ought to be praying more often. We ought to ask God what His will is for a family." Norma and I concurred: "That's a great idea!"

We didn't prioritize anything; we just put ideas down in whatever order they were mentioned. We kept brainstorming and talking until we had five things that everyone agreed would really be good for our family.

Then I said, "The Scripture says to honor your mother and father and obey them. No complaining, no whining." We found other passages about children obeying their parents, and we attached a verse to each of the five items in our constitution. Each of the kids agreed to honor and obey God by honoring and obeying Mom and Dad. For example, they were going to say, "Yes, ma'am" and "Yes, sir" when we asked them to do something, and they weren't going to give us a hassle. And when they asked us if they could do something and we said no, they weren't going to whine and complain and make life miserable.

Another clause in our constitution allowed our kids to call for a council meeting anytime they thought we parents were doing something unfair. If they wanted to, they could bring an "attorney": they could bring their friends with them to any family meeting. (Through the years, we probably had only five council meetings.)

Also, since Norma and I wanted the kids to feel highly honored, the only time we ever spanked them was when they were egregiously dishonoring to one another or to us. Every member of the family knew what Romans 12:10 says: "Be devoted to one another in brotherly love. Honor one another above yourselves." We recognized and believed that honoring others was very important. Now we had to live that way.

GET ALL THE FACTS

Usually when I sensed that the kids thought something was unfair, I stopped immediately as a way of honoring them, and I would say, "Give me the facts here because, for your sake, I don't want to goof this up."

One time, for example, I walked into the kitchen and saw Greg fling his paper plate full of food across the counter at Kari. When it reached the intended target, chips, a sandwich, and applesauce splattered all over her—and she was furious. (She was around twelve years old, and he was nine or ten at the time.)

Having walked in just in time to see the plate hit Kari, I grabbed Greg and said, "That was very dishonoring to your sister."

I was going to march him upstairs to his room, but he broke in: "Hold on, hold on. I need to break into a council meeting here."

"What?" I asked, surprised.

He continued, "You don't know what happened just before that."

And I responded, "You're right. I don't."

So I sat down at the table with both of them, and I found out that Norma had asked Kari to make Greg's lunch. Kari had made it, but Greg had already eaten. Not knowing he had already eaten, she retorted, "Well, you're eating this whether you like it or not," and she just flipped it over to him.

Of course, it hit him, and he quipped back, "Hey, I said I'm not eating this. I'm not hungry." And he flipped it back to her—and that's when I walked in. I didn't catch the part where he said he wasn't hungry and she said he was going to eat it anyway, so I hadn't had all the facts.

Then Kari told her side of the story: "Dad, Mom said to make Greg's lunch. I didn't know he'd already eaten. I was just carrying out Mom's orders. He wasn't going to eat, but I told him, 'Yes, you are, because Mom said I'm supposed to feed you.'" Kari felt she was doing her job by obeying Mom, but she wasn't really listening to Greg.

After we got the facts straight, we laughed together. Kari underscored her point, "Dad, I was just real frustrated with him. He was being cocky."

"Okay. I get it," I said, and we all high-fived each other, and that was the end of it.

Your kids will flat-out reject everything about
you if they see you being inconsistent.

YOU HAVE TO BE REAL

Part of honoring others is being genuine. Your kids will flat-out reject everything about you, especially if you're a believer in Christ, if they see you being inconsistent. Kids are very alert to that kind of thing. When our kids saw that I was the same person at home that I was when I was out speaking or doing films or appearing on TV, that what I was doing was real and genuine, that realization had a significant positive effect on their lives.

Let your kids help you by pointing out your inconsistencies. For example, they might say, "You tell us not to swear, but we hear you swearing all the time." And then there was an example from our family that I still remember vividly.

We were driving through the high country of the Southwest and stopped at a Pizza Hut in some little town in the middle of nowhere. The sign said: "All-You-Can-Eat Salad." Norma ordered the salad, and I ordered something else. We had little money back then, so I didn't order the salad. I just had a few bites of Norma's.

The teenage server saw me eat from Norma's salad plate, so she came over and said, "Sir, you're not allowed to eat your wife's salad. It's all you can eat for one person, not the family."

Her comment irritated the life out of me! I was tired from driving, and I don't like to be controlled anyway. Furthermore, I thought it was ridiculous for this young woman to come over and correct me. What did it really matter? I wasn't eating that much, I reasoned. Well, I went after her verbally. I got so upset that my lower back tightened up, and I had to consciously calm myself down because I knew that I could have a heart attack.

As we drove off, I wasn't speaking to anybody. Greg finally offered, "Dad, are you going to let that teenager rob you and our family of the good day we could be having?"

"Yeah. You're right," I said.

Then he continued: "Dad, how honoring were you to that girl?" Greg's question brought me up short. Had we not been so many miles away, I probably would have turned around, gone back to Pizza Hut, and asked the server's forgiveness. Greg was right: I hadn't been very honoring to her. And that, after all, was the family rule.

Of course, Norma spoke up immediately and said, "That's right, Dad. That's the rule, and we should have obeyed it." Yes, I had blown it.

A WORD OF WARNING

Honoring our children can sometimes be time consuming. Parents need to know their kids' personalities and be prepared for long discussions with some of them. For example, when Greg disagreed with me, it was sometimes a two-hour discussion—a two-hour exercise in honoring him—before we came to a conclusion. Honoring Michael and Kari was much faster: our discussions would be over in five minutes.

Children with strong personalities like Greg notice everything. Michael and Kari might overlook a lot of stuff, but not Greg. He is consistent, like his mom. If I said something to him, then I'd better be living it.

*Children with strong personalities
notice everything.*

Incidentally, Greg is my main mentor today. That's how valuable he is in my life. With the things he has learned in his marriage intensives, he has even helped his mother and me in our marriage.

Michael is another one of my key mentors. By the way, he donated a kidney to me nine years ago. He says to me all the time, "Hey, just remember I'm keeping you alive with my kidney. I'm still in pain, and you're not." But he says he'd go through the whole thing again. That's definitely an expression of his honoring me.

Suppose, though, our relationship over the years had been less than warm and harmonious, and he didn't sense he was very important to me. How willing would he have been to say, "Yeah, I'll step up to the plate, go into surgery, and risk my life for you"?

Michael, in fact, did almost die on the operating table. He was in critical condition after he donated his kidney because they hit his lungs and his lung collapsed. Michael truly was willing to lay down his life for me. But again, if he'd been angry with me and had never felt honored, he might have said, "You know what? Get a kidney from somebody else." Most likely, he wouldn't even have been tested to see if he was a match.

Of course we aren't to honor others for selfish reasons. You don't raise kids for future body parts! But Michael's sacrifice is definitely an example of extreme honor.

THE RESULT OF HONORING

A family will suffer certain consequences if honoring one another isn't valued. In fact, when our kids were young, I was really bothered by what was going on between them. I knew it was normal for brothers and sisters to sometimes be upset with one another. But all I could think of was those families who are in a big mess when they get together for holidays. They don't get along, and they're hostile to one another. I didn't want that for my family when my kids were grown up, but I could see that they were heading in that direction if we didn't do something while they were still young.

Needless to say, I'm so glad that I had a wise and godly doctor who shared with me his secret to healthy families—and that Norma and I listened and chose to act on his advice. Keep honor high and anger low—this goal has worked well for the Smalley family.

Gary Smalley is one of the country's best-known authors and speakers on marriage and family relationships. He is the president and founder of the Smalley Relationship Center, which provides research, relationship coaching, nationwide conferences, books, videos, and small-group curricula. Gary and his wife, Norma, have been married for forty-seven years and live in Branson, Missouri. They have three married children—Kari, Greg, and Michael—and ten grandchildren.

12

Learn!

Cynthia Ulrich Tobias

I think the best parenting advice I ever got was from my dad, and it's just one word.

I started hearing it as a child, and I heard it until I was well into young adulthood. Through those years, I actually thought the word was meant to frustrate me, but as I look back, I now understand how that one word has shaped my entire life's work. The word? *Learn.*

"Dad, I want to speak Spanish."

"That's a good idea, Cindy."

"But I don't know how."

"Well, *learn.*"

"How can I learn if I don't know how?"

"You'll figure it out."

Why wouldn't my dad just *help* me? Why did he have to make it so hard? As a child, I was puzzled by "Well, *learn.*" As a teenager, I was often exasperated by that remark. Then, when I became a parent, my dad's standard response to my interest in something suddenly made a lot of sense to me.

First of all, let me make it clear that my dad was always there for me—and I knew it. He encouraged me, motivated me, and praised me. But he refused to do things for me when there was an opportunity for me to do it myself—or to learn to do it myself.

Let me also make it clear that I wasn't exactly the easiest child to work with. My strong will and independent spirit (both inherited from my father) presented consistent challenges for my mom and dad. But they were determined to instill in me a love for God, a desire to succeed, and a heart for service to others. Oh, and the invaluable skill of *learning*.

I heard my dad's frequent reminder that I should *learn* as his vote of confidence in me as well as a challenge. He obviously had faith in my ability to gain the knowledge I needed, and he refused to let me shrug my shoulders and give up when he knew I was capable of overcoming any obstacle in my path.

*I heard my dad's frequent reminder that
I should* learn *as his vote of confidence
in me as well as a challenge.*

My younger sister Sandee was just the opposite of me. She was naturally a more compliant child and a serious and traditional student who usually earned better grades than

I did. She got along with pretty much everyone, and she virtually never challenged authority or questioned parental directives. Dad seemed to know he needed to deal with Sandee differently than he did with me. She craved specific instructions and happily took advice and warnings to heart. (I think God must have been giving my parents a much-deserved break after five years of dealing with me!)

GIVE KIDS ROOM TO FIGURE IT OUT

My folks insist they didn't pray for this to happen, but God later gave me my own strong-willed child, and my dad's example turned out to be one of his greatest gifts to me as a parent. My twin boys, Mike and Robert, were both bright and full of energy from the beginning, but I quickly realized that Mike was going to be a real challenge. Even as a toddler, he resisted my attempts to insist he do things my way. I knew it was essential to maintain my parental authority, and I took great pains to make sure I kept my children safe and taught them strong moral and spiritual values. But I could already see how critical it was going to be to give Mike room to figure out some things on his own.

I was blessed to have my mom provide daycare for the boys from the time they were infants until they started school. My dad was retired by then, and my parents turned their home into one big educational wonderland. We put toddler-level teaching posters all along the hallway walls and let the boys decide what they were most interested in. Whenever a boy pointed to a poster and asked, "What's that?" we happily gave him as much information as he wanted. Right away we saw the differences in what the boys were drawn to. Rob gravitated toward posters of community helpers and families, while Mike was fascinated by the solar system and historical figures.

When the boys started school, they continued to explore their world beyond the classroom. We delighted in watching them express their curiosity and pursue their interests in addition to learning what was required in the classroom. Thanks to my dad, I was aware of the infinite value of encouraging children to *learn* how to do things rather than simply showing them how something is done.

CREATE A DESIRE TO LEARN

I believe that, as parents, we should be continually creating in our children a desire to learn and providing them the means to do so. At the same time—especially for our strong-willed kids—we should resist the urge to simply do things for them. Granted, it's much easier to just tie the shoe when you're in a hurry than to take the time to let your child figure it out. When the deadline is looming and the homework isn't complete, it's tempting to just sit down with your procrastinating student and get it done.

But what happens to the incredibly important task of teaching our children to take responsibility for their own success? If we direct every step, supply every instruction, and monitor every movement, how will they learn to be on their own? Of course there has to be a balance. Encouraging children to learn on their own must be tempered by retaining parental authority and ensuring thoughtful supervision. But there's something powerful and profound in our children learning to *learn*, and watching them explore the possibilities according to their own design and strengths.

If we direct every step, supply every instruction, and monitor every movement, how will our children learn to be on their own?

GUIDE THEM INTO LEARNING

Occasions for disciplining my sons also taught me about the power of learning. Mike quickly put up defenses and barriers when I talked to him about something he did wrong. As a strong-willed child myself, I know that the last thing kids want to hear is a phrase like "What lesson have you learned from this?" But I discovered that if I used questions carefully, Mike almost always learned from his own assessment of the situation.

Case in point: The boys attended a Christian school with a very strong code of ethics and a number of rules that Mike sometimes considered too restrictive. One afternoon he came home with a detention slip he had earned because of his disrespectful behavior. I resisted my impulse to scold and remind him how he should act. Instead I calmly asked him a few questions.

"Mike, what were you trying to accomplish?"

"Mom, the new principal just doesn't treat us with any respect—but he demands that we show respect to *him*. I just thought I could start a protest and others would join me to object to the treatment we're getting."

"How did it work?" I asked.

Mike's shoulders drooped, and he shook his head. "Not like I expected," he admitted. What followed was a conversation about what he would do differently if he could and how being new to the school might be presenting some pretty intense challenges for the principal. I asked Mike what he thought his next step should be, and he told me it was his plan to apologize to the principal and figure out a way to work things out.

Our discussion of a situation doesn't always end up like that, but I'm amazed how many times it does. There's something about being *guided* into learning instead of being forced to recite a lesson that gives a child a healthy sense of ownership and responsibility. And one of the biggest benefits is how much this approach to a situation can strengthen your relationship with each other.

My dad celebrated his eighty-sixth birthday this year, and he's still a powerful and positive influence in my life. I continue to learn from him, and I seek him out for advice and comfort. It's my prayer that my boys will do the same with me. We've encouraged them to explore their world, and they are blossoming into wonderful young adults. They are eager for each new experience, and there's one word in their vocabulary they embrace with great pleasure and anticipation: *learn!*

---❧---

Cynthia Ulrich Tobias is founder, manager, and CEO of AppLe St. (Applied Learning Styles). She is an author and speaker, known throughout the United States and internationally for her enter-taining, practical, and life-changing presentations. She is also the best-selling author of The Way They Learn, The Way We Work, Every Child Can Succeed, Bringing Out the Best in Your Child, *and* I Hate School! *Cynthia is the mother of twin sons, who are now in college.*

13

Let's Faith-Talk!

Mark A. Holmen

I was recently boarding my plane to spend thirteen days on a speaking tour across New Zealand. I was communicating with my daughter the way most dads communicate with their teenagers today: through text messaging. As the flight crew began preparing for takeoff, I sent my daughter a final text: "Time to go. Know that I will miss you a ton, love you even more, and will be praying for you continuously." Then—just before I shut off my phone—I received the following text back from her: "Love you too, Daddy. May the Lord bless you and keep you. May He make His face shine on you and be gracious to you. May He look upon you with favor and give you peace."

If Moses has known about texting, he probably would have included it in his Deuteronomy 6:7 instructions, which is the best parenting advice I've ever found. In that passage Moses is very clear: "Impress [the commands of God] on your children. Talk about them when you sit at home and when you walk along the road, when you lie down and when you get up." It is by intentionally and consistently talking to our children about God and His ways that we encourage our kids to live in a loving and lifelong relationship with Him.

It is by intentionally and consistently talking to our children about God and His ways that we encourage our kids to live in a loving and lifelong relationship with Him.

For this reason I have not only trained my daughter at home, but I have also given my life to being a full-time author, speaker, and missionary for the Faith at Home movement. I travel the world speaking to church leaders and parents about the importance of reestablishing the home as the primary place where faith is taught, lived, expressed, and nurtured. That begins with training parents to talk to their kids about the ways of God when they sit at home, when they walk along the road, when they lie down, and when they get up—and when they text or email.

I'm not sure when, why, or how it happened, but somehow as parents we have fallen away from doing this very important aspect of Christian parenting. We can talk to our kids about sports, school, and extracurricular activities, yet when it comes to talking to our kids about God and His ways, we have some serious work to do. In 1990, Search

Institute released the results of a nationwide survey of more than eleven thousand participants from five hundred sixty-one congregations across six different denominations, and the numbers were revealing:

- Only 12 percent of the teenagers surveyed had a regular dialogue with their mother on faith or life issues.
- Only 5 percent of those teenagers had a regular dialogue with their father on faith or life issues.[1]

In 2003, researcher George Barna confirmed these numbers while he was working on his book *Transforming Children Into Spiritual Champions*: "We discovered in a typical week, fewer than 10 percent of parents who regularly attend church with their kids read the Bible together, pray together (other than at meal times) or participate in an act of service as a family unit."[2]

WHERE FAITH IS NURTURED

My friend and mentor Dr. Roland Martinson once said, "What we ought to do is let the kids drop their parents off at church. Train the parents and then send them back into their mission fields, their homes, to grow Christians!"

If we want our children to have a lasting faith in Jesus Christ, then faith talk needs to be a part of our everyday life with them, not just an hour a week on Sunday mornings. Yet faith talk is just not happening today. In an attempt to change this situation, let's use the word *TRAIN* as an acronym for some guidelines, and you'll see how you can establish or reestablish faith talk with your children.

*If we want our children to have a lasting
faith in Jesus Christ, then faith talk needs to
be a part of our everyday life with them.*

T = TIME

When is the right time for faith talk? One question I consistently hear from parents is this: "When am I going to find the time to engage in faith talk or devotions with my kids?" Many moms and dads feel that they need to carve out a specific time each day or week to bring the entire family together for a time of faith talk, a time when everyone is sitting still at the kitchen table and behaving, with a candle burning and the Bible open. Now don't get me wrong! If you are able to pull this off, then I say to you, "Well done, good and faithful servant!" But all I can say is, in the home of my youth, that would only have made us kids less interested in conversations integrating faith and life. Knowing this, my parents never led us in a time of formal devotions. Instead they simply seized teachable moments and engaged us in faith talk right then.

For example, when I was growing up and we would see an accident on the side of the road, my dad or mom would simply say, "Let's take a moment right now to pray for the people who were in that accident." My point is simply this:

instead of trying to create a time for faith talk, seize the times and opportunities for faith talk that God provides on a day-to-day, moment-by-moment, basis. For example, if you see a rainbow in the sky, ask your kids to recall the promises God wants us to remember, and that will become a time of faith talk or devotions.

R = REPETITION

Another key to establishing faith talk is *repetition*. The word *deuteronomy* means "repetition of the law." If you read the entire book of Deuteronomy, you'll find that Moses continually repeated the basic commands of God to a very stubborn group of people who wanted to live life their way instead of God's way. (Does that sound familiar?) In the same way, faith talk will be repetitious as we consistently talk about the ways of God to our children.

Even when our kids say, "I know what you're going to say, Dad," say it again because in a world where everything else is constantly changing, it's vital that our children realize that the ways of God do not change. For example, my wife has blessed our daughter every night of her life by praying our version of Numbers 6:24–26 over her: "May the Lord bless you and keep you. May He make His face shine on you and be gracious to you. May He look upon you with favor and give you peace. In the name of the Father, Son, and Holy Spirit. We love you. Amen." Now sixteen, my daughter will not go to bed without receiving that blessing from my wife, and before I travel, my daughter prays that same blessing over me. Faith talk's truths gain power and significance with repetition.

A = ACCEPTANCE

Unfortunately, one of the consistent complaints I hear when leading parenting events is "I wish my husband would . . . I wish my wife would . . . I wish our family were more like . . ." Friends, one of the keys with faith talk is *accepting* that we are all going to do it differently. And if you have more than one child, you are going to need to accept that the way you engage in faith talk is probably going to have to be different with each child. In other words, how and when you engage in faith talk will be different for husband and wife, and it will also be different with each of your children.

> *If you have more than one child, you are going to need to accept that the way you engage in faith talk is probably going to have to be different with each child.*

For example, my father-in-law is a strong person of faith, yet he didn't engage in many formal faith talks with my wife when she was growing up. Yet every night as she walked past his bedroom, she peeked inside. And every night she saw him on his knees in prayer. That's how he spent the last twenty minutes before he went to bed. Now I could sit here and judgmentally say, "He should have . . ." but the fact is that while he didn't do other things, what he did do—his modeling—spoke to my wife. Today, her favorite position for prayer is on her knees. So let's accept that faith talk can occur in a wide variety of ways.

I = INTENTIONALITY

Another reality about faith talk is recognizing that at times we have to *intentionally* make it happen. Sometimes we'll need to close the bedroom door, pull the car off to the side of road, or—and this is true—kick the ladder down from the rooftop so that faith talk can happen.

My father-in-law kicked the ladder down from the rooftop when, after a rough first year of college, my wife went home and announced that she had decided not to go back to school. Instead, she was going to live at home and work at Dairy King. (Her small Iowa hometown wasn't big enough to have a Dairy *Queen*.) A couple of days later, Maria was lying out in the sun enjoying her early retirement at age nineteen while my father-in-law was working on the roof of the garage. He asked her to come up and help him work on the roof. She climbed the ladder to the rooftop, he told her to sit down, and when she was seated, he kicked the ladder to the ground! He then sat down next to her and said, "I think it's time we have a little talk about your decision regarding college."

What my wife remembers most about that time on the roof (although she will never forget the ladder incident) was the conversation they had and that her dad cared enough to listen and talk.

Friends, at times we are going to need to *make* faith talk happen. Rather than shy away from those opportunities, let's do whatever it takes to make those conversations happen, trusting that God will do a great work in and through them even if they don't seem easy at first.

N = NEVER-ENDING

The final aspect of faith talk is that it needs to *never end*: we need to consistently and continually find ways to engage in faith talk with our kids no matter what age they are. I'm quite clear with grandparents that there is no retirement plan when it comes to engaging in faith talk with their children and grandchildren, and I conclude by saying, "You can stop when Satan stops."

As our kids grow, we simply need to be more creative about how we engage in faith talk. With my sixteen-year-old daughter, my primary ways are text messaging and talking in the car on the way to or from school. My wife writes notes to her on her lunch bags, and I am also using a Bible app to send her Scripture verses each day. Faith talk is to never end.

There you have it, friends. Let's engage in faith talk with our children anytime and all the time. As our conversations about God happen casually and naturally, truths about Him become impressed on our children's hearts.

1. Reprinted with permission from "Effective Christian Education: A National Study of Protestant Congregations." Copyright © 1990 by Search Institute SM. No other use is permitted without prior permission from Search Institute, 615 First Avenue NE, Minneapolis, MN 55413; www.search-institute.org.

2. George Barna, *Transforming Children into Spiritual Champions: Why Children Should Be Your Church's #1 Priority* (Ventura, CA: Regal Books, 2003), 78.

Mark Holmen is a national and international consultant and speaker for Faith At Home, a movement that equips congregations to make the home the primary place where faith is nurtured. Mark served as the senior pastor of Ventura Missionary Church until recently, when he stepped down to pursue full-time ministry with Faith at Home. Mark and his wife, Maria, have one daughter, Malyn. For more information about Mark Holmen, visit www.faithathome.com.

14

Parenting from the Inside Out

Vicki Courtney

As a recent empty nester, I have the luxury of looking back on the parenting wisdom I have heard over the years and evaluating which tidbits of truth mattered the most. If I had to pinpoint one bit of advice that stuck with me through the years of parenting our three children, it would be this: *parent from the inside out.*

I learned the nuts and bolts of this principle at a parenting event led by Dr. David Ferguson, who coauthored *Intimate Encounters* (a fabulous marriage workbook) and *Parenting with Intimacy* (an equally fabulous parenting workbook). At the time, my children were young and I was adept at "fixing things." In other words, when my children misbehaved, I focused on *fixing the behavior* rather than diving into the heart of the matter to discover what might be *causing the behavior.* I kept things prettied up on the outside just in case the Joneses were watching.

GETTING TO THE HEART OF THE MATTER

Quite frankly, parenting the behavior is much easier and less time consuming than parenting the heart. For example, when my daughter was in grade school, I once rewarded her with a pack of gum for good behavior. When she got home, her brother asked her for a piece. "No way! It's my gum," she proclaimed. Long story short, without parent intervention, she wasn't about to share her gum.

Quite frankly, parenting the behavior is much easier and less time consuming than parenting the heart.

Reminding my daughter that I had bought the gum, I told her to give her brother a piece or I'd confiscate the entire pack of gum and do it myself.

My goal at the time was to simply modify the behavior and solve the immediate problem. Oh, I could get her to comply with the rules, but the results wouldn't likely be long-term. Parenting from the inside out would mean taking the time to sit down with my daughter and find out why she didn't want to share her gum.

So I took my daughter aside and asked her. Her reason was simple—and quite predictable: She just didn't feel like it. She wanted the gum all to herself, every smacking piece of it. (No pun intended.) At the heart of the matter, my daughter was simply being *selfish*. Imagine that.

Psalm 26:2–3 says, "Test me, O LORD, and try me, examine my heart and my mind; for your love is ever before me, and I walk continually in your truth." Too often, we worry more about behavior modification tactics than diving down deep to the root of the sin problem. And selfishness is a sin.

After spending some time talking with my daughter about the sin of selfishness and God's view of sin, I encouraged her to examine her heart and run her actions past God. Of course I assured her that we all sin and fall short of the glory of God (even grown-ups!), and I reminded her of God's love and forgiveness.

EXAMINING THE HEART

As our children get older, the spiritual stakes will get higher. Not sharing a pack of gum is the least of our worries when our children hit the teen years and are tempted to drink at a party or hook up with their crush.

I recall the time I discovered that my youngest son— who was then in high school—had been out drinking with his Christian friends. My first instinct was to ground him from everything imaginable and put him on total lockdown to discourage the behavior in the future.

He did get grounded, but his father and I also spent a great deal of time helping him figure out his motives. What had led to his drinking? (His answers were typical: curiosity, wanting to fit in, and so on.) Then we asked him if he had experienced any conviction for his actions, and much to our relief, he opened up and shared how it was difficult for him to approach God after his sin. Tears of sorrow followed as he explained how he felt like he was living a double life. He even said, "I'm glad I got caught." We reminded our son of God's counsel to "come boldly to the throne of grace" (Hebrews 4:16, NKJV) and that no sin is too big for the forgiveness of God.

That incident gave rise to a new practice in our home. Before, as my teenagers headed out the door with car keys in hand, I would shout out a friendly reminder: "I love you! Make good choices!" But as I learned to focus more on heart examination than behavior modification, I realized that the key to making good choices is to first *remember the cross.* So after that unfortunate situation with my son, whenever he left the house, I would call out, "I love you! RTC!" Because of the many conversations we'd had about the importance of heart examination and the need to remember the cross, my son knew exactly what I meant.

GOING A STEP FURTHER

This valuable bit of wisdom—*parent from the inside out*— has appeared in many of the parenting books and Bible studies I've written as well as in messages I've shared across the country. Case in point: When speaking to teenage girls about modesty, I can simply share God's perspective from 1 Timothy 2:9—"I also want women to dress modestly, with decency and propriety"—and leave it at that. The problem is solved, and most girls will leave the event with a renewed zeal to clean out their closets when they get home. (Yeah, right!)

Or I can go a step further by letting these young women know *what* God has to say on the topic of modesty (1 Timothy 2:9) and encouraging them to ask God to examine their hearts (Psalm 26:2–3) and show them *why* they, like so many Christian girls, choose to dress immodestly. Are they insecure and desperate for male attention, so desperate, in fact, that they are willing to settle for the wrong kind of attention? Or might they just be followers, looking to fit in by wearing the latest trends? Either way, dressing immodestly is a symptom of a deeper root problem, and if immodesty is not addressed at the core, it will likely continue, even if these young women do take temporary measures and clean out their closets.

The Hebrew word for *examine* in Psalm 26:2 is *shaphat* (shaw-fat'), which means "to judge" as in "to pass sentence for or against." Another translation says it this way: "Put me on trial, Lord, and cross-examine me. Test my motives and my heart. For I am always aware of your unfailing love, and I have lived according to your truth" (NLT). The idea of asking God to put our hearts on trial can be a bit unsettling, so it's important that we know God's purpose in examining our hearts. The Hebrew word for *try* (as in "try my heart") is *tsaraph* (tsaw-raf´), which means to "refine; melt; purge away," much like a goldsmith does when purifying gold. Of course, we can hardly expect our children to put their hearts on trial unless we ourselves are implementing the practice in our own lives. When our children know that we too are sinners saved by grace and that we are actively laying our hearts bare before God, they will understand that we are all works in progress.

REMEMBERING THE CROSS

When our children sin, we can't force them to experience true "godly sorrow" that in turn leads to sincere repentance (2 Corinthians 7:10). However, we can pray that God will work in their hearts when they stray, and we can encourage them to regularly and consistently examine their motives. Ralph Waldo Emerson once wrote, "God enters by a private door into every individual." We can't put a deadbolt on the doors of our hearts. Yet, truth be told, many Christians spend more energy attempting to barricade the secret places of their hearts and tuning out the Judge's verdict regarding their underlying motives and affections. Only those who *want* to be refined will ask God to purge away the impurities that lie deep within their hearts.

> *When our children sin, we can't force*
> *them to experience true "godly sorrow."*
> *However, we can pray that God will*
> *work in their hearts when they stray.*

We need to understand that God judges our motives and affections as an act of His unfailing love for us and that we are to keep that love "ever before" us (Psalm 26:3). Only then can we walk continually in God's truth. The same is true for our children. When they misbehave, we can employ trendy behavior modification tactics gleaned from the latest best-selling parenting book, or we can go a step further and encourage a heart examination that is more likely to result in godly sorrow—the kind of godly sorrow that leads to repentance. Parenting from the inside out—examining our hearts and remembering the cross (RTC!)—is key to a true change in behavior.

Vicki Courtney is a speaker and best-selling author of numerous books and Bible studies, including 5 Conversations You Must Have with Your Daughter *and* 5 Conversations You Must Have with Your Son. *She and her husband, Keith, have been married twenty-five years and have three grown children and one grandchild. They live in Austin, Texas, with their children nearby. For more about Vicki, visit VickiCourtney.com.*

15

Kids May Hear What You Say, But They Believe What You Do

Jerry B. Jenkins

About a year after Dianna and I were married, I heard a bit of advice that changed the rest of my life. As a young journalist, I was assigned to interview people for a Sunday school paper. In a matter of just a few weeks, I interviewed five men and heard five very different stories. Yet they shared something in common: each was a Christian husband and father roughly twice my age.

In the course of my interviews, I asked each if he had any regrets at this stage of his life. To a man, every one of them told me he wished he'd spent more time with his kids while they were growing up. Some had prodigals. Some were estranged from their children. Others felt their relationships were strained at best.

One said, "I told them they were my priority, but my schedule told them otherwise. You know, they hear what you say, but they believe what you do."

After the fifth time I heard a father's regret, I told my wife, "God's clearly trying to tell me something. If I have those same regrets when I'm that age, I'll be without excuse."

Dianna nodded. "We need to make sure that doesn't happen."

A NEW FAMILY POLICY

That evening we established a policy we promised to remember when we had kids of our own: We decided that I would do no freelance writing or any work from the office from the time I got home every day until the kids went to bed. So sometimes we put them to bed at 4:30 in the afternoon. (Not really.)

When our first son, Dallas, was born, we put our policy into action. The moment I got home, I took over parenting. I changed him, fed him, rocked him, sang to him, read Scripture to him, and put him to bed. In the night I took my turn tending to him.

I was there when Dallas rolled over for the first time, began to crawl, pulled himself up, said his first words, and took his first steps. He was a cuddler, a lover, a hugger, and I enjoyed few things more than gathering him in and holding him close.

Our policy helped Dianna too. Mothering a toddler all day long is an exhausting, demanding job. She needed time to herself, for her chores and hobbies and interests. Today she tells me that my immersion into fatherhood not only freed her, but also made her feel honored.

BUSY GETS BUSIER

Dallas was a busy, verbal, active two-and-a-half-year-old when Chad was born. Now the real fun began. Dallas stayed close, watched, and helped in his own way as I did for Chad all that I had done for him. And part of the ritual became putting both boys to bed.

For the new baby, that meant changing, feeding, rocking, singing, and putting him down when he fell asleep. For Dallas, it meant climbing into bed with him, reading to him, helping him memorize Bible verses, and just talking.

Five years later Mike came along, and by now the rituals had been set. Were there times when I regretted the policy? No. Not once. Sure, I had a lot of work to do. I was an executive with a large Christian organization, and my workday didn't always end when I left the office. Plus, I was a freelance author, writing several books a year on my own time.

And when exactly was "my own time"? I followed the policy religiously. For several hours a day, I invested my time in my sons. No closed doors. No research. No writing. No office work. No TV. I didn't have to tell my sons they were my priority. They knew nothing else.

By 9:00 PM, when all three boys were finally in bed and I'd spent time with Dianna, I did my writing or caught up on office work. I'm a morning person, but I had no choice.

Somehow I was more productive than ever because I was forced to redeem those few hours before my own bedtime.

SETTING AN EXAMPLE

Dallas and Chad saw Mike go from newborn to infant to toddler to school kid. And I marveled at how different the three of them were. Dallas was the talker, Chad, the quiet one, and Mike, a combination.

My time was theirs. If they wanted to talk, we talked. If they wanted to not talk, we didn't talk. Play, work, study, watch TV together—whatever they wanted to do, we did. Sometimes they merely wanted to climb on me.

As the boys grew older, my several hours each day with them became more and more precious. The highlight of every evening was getting them to bed—going to each one's room and singing our songs, reciting our verses, and talking.

I was there when each one received Christ as his Savior. Needless to say, I wouldn't trade those experiences for anything this world has to offer.

I became known in the neighborhood as the one father who was always outside playing with his kids. Dianna told me neighborhood children would sometimes knock on the door and ask if I could come out and play. I was a novelty, and I loved every minute of it.

When we moved to the country, I built a baseball diamond on our property where we logged hours and days and years. All three boys were involved in local sports almost year-round, and I don't remember missing a soccer, basketball, or baseball game.

PRECIOUS MEMORIES

- When Dallas was about six, he was playing under the kitchen table, lecturing a *Star Wars* action figure. He was unaware that Dianna and I were in the next room and could hear everything he was saying. He said, "You may die in this mission. You don't want to go to hell, because Satan's mean and he won't give you anything. But if you go to heaven, you can ask Jesus for anything you want. And if it's okay with your mom, He'll give it to you."
- When Chad was about five, he asked me to weigh him. So I put him on the scale and told him how much he weighed. He said, "Let's see how much you weigh, Dad." I was reluctant because then I weighed more than a hundred pounds more than I do now, but I climbed aboard, and we watched the numbers whiz by. Chad said, "Hey, Dad, you weigh all of it!"
- When Mike was in sixth grade, his basketball team lost. He said, "It wasn't fair. The other team had a player with hair under his arms."

    I said, "That doesn't seem fair. How old was that kid?"

    Mike said, "They told us he was only twelve but that he's already been through poverty."

My heart breaks for parents who raised their kids with priorities similar to Dianna's and mine, yet saw their children rebel and turn from the church and the faith. I can't say our policy is the reason we never faced such rebellion and the reason our kids are our best friends to this day. But I do know that, having seen all three boys grow to honorable manhood, all three graduate from Christian colleges, all three loving and serving God, and two of them raising great kids of their own, I wouldn't change a thing.

QUALITY IS QUANTITY

Some years back, a myth swept through the church, and it went roughly like this: If you don't have a lot of time to spend with your kids, make sure the time you do spend with them is quality time.

That was a lie from the pit and something too many parents used to justify spending less time with their children. To kids, quality time *is* quantity time.

To kids, quality time is quantity time.

One of the highlights of my life came when one of my sons told me about when he and a bunch of college teammates sat in a circle sharing stories about their relationships with their fathers. Every kid, it seemed, had horrible memories, regrets, and unmended tears in their relationship.

"When they got to me," my son said, "I just said, 'I guess I had a better dad than I even realized. He was always there and he always loved me. I've got no bad stories to share.'"

No award, no review, no royalty check, no best-selling book could come within a light-year of a priceless treasure like that.

Tell your kids they're your priority—but then prove it. They'll hear what you say, but they'll believe what you do.

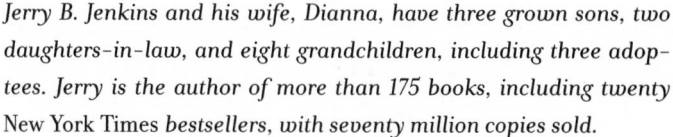

Jerry B. Jenkins and his wife, Dianna, have three grown sons, two daughters-in-law, and eight grandchildren, including three adoptees. Jerry is the author of more than 175 books, including twenty New York Times *bestsellers, with seventy million copies sold.*

16

The Challenge of Parenting as a Team

Juli Slattery

Maybe you've heard this old saying about marriage that the late Larry Burkett quoted: "If the two of you are alike, one of you is unnecessary."[1] This bit of wisdom relates to all areas of marriage, but it has meant the most to me in the context of parenting.

My husband, Mike, and I are definitely an example of opposites attracting. As much as I was drawn toward his laid-back surfer mentality when we were dating, learning to parent three boys with him has, at times, been a challenge. We began with different ideas about discipline, what to feed them, and how many episodes of VeggieTales a day is okay for a three-year-old. Now Mike and I are navigating the teen years with dissimilar views on dating, cell phones, and curfews.

Yes, parenting as a team is a challenge. There have been seasons when I felt resentful that Mike was the pizza-and-a-movie guy while I was known for serving broccoli and encouraging the boys to read classics. One day, Mike jokingly taught the boys to chant, "A vote for Daddy is a vote for fun!" Even though he meant it in a light spirit, I wasn't so happy about being painted as Mom the Party Pooper. Don't get me wrong. In some areas of parenting, Mike is far stricter than I am. The former Marine definitely comes out when it's time for room inspection!

As a psychologist, though, I know that a united front between Mom and Dad is essential to good parenting. Yet as a woman, I sometimes have a hard time being united with my polar-opposite husband. But Mike and I have had an easier time working together as a team since we began to embrace the truth of Larry Burkett's statement. God brought us together with all of our differences, not to frustrate us but to complement each other in our parenting efforts. Our boys need both a mom and a dad. Beyond that, they can richly benefit from having parents who are so different in personality.

God brought my husband and I together with all of our differences, not to frustrate us but to complement each other in our parenting efforts.

Almost every couple will encounter some differences in how they approach parenting, and those differences can either polarize the two of them or bring balance to the family. When a husband and wife become polarized, they each become more extreme in their styles in an attempt—conscious or otherwise—to counteract the other. For example, permissive Mom lets the kids get away with murder as she compensates for how strict Dad is. When Dad sees Mom being permissive, he reacts by creating and enforcing even more rules for the kids. When parents get caught in this cycle of reacting and polarizing, their differences will erode the foundation of their parenting.

So, how do you begin to actually work as a team in spite of your differences?

EMBRACING HUMILITY

The first step is a difficult one: embrace humility. Philippians 2:3 says to act in humility, to "consider others better than yourselves." Differences will divide you when you cling to the belief that your way is the best way. Even if you would never say that out loud, you undoubtedly maintain your parenting personality because you believe it works better than your spouse's approach. It takes genuine humility to admit and accept that you have something to learn from your husband or wife.

Choosing an attitude of humility has taken an extra amount of God's grace for me because the fancy degree and title behind my name proclaims that I am a "family expert."

What could I possibly learn from Mike, a 401(k) specialist? As it turns out, quite a lot. In fact, I am discovering that Mike is right on parenting issues just about as often as I am. There have been many times that, in hindsight, I see how his perspective was wiser than mine. I can become overly empathetic toward our sons at times when they actually need some tough love. I am learning to ask the Lord for humility so I can see my limitations and lean on my husband's strength.

LEARNING DISCERNMENT

In addition to humility, we parents need the discernment to know what is a mountain and what is a molehill. Not every parenting issue you disagree on is worth taking a stand for. In the heat of the moment, every minor decision seems important, but the rearview mirror shows that many prove rather insignificant.

It was Halloween and my oldest son, Michael, was four years old. It was the first time he was old enough to go trick-or-treating in our neighborhood. His costume was ready, and I was feeding him an early dinner. Mike came home from work to Michael and me debating about whether he had to finish his spinach. Mike was tired and unilaterally announced that Michael would not go trick-or-treating if he didn't finish his dinner. When Michael chose not to eat his spinach, I was devastated—and pretty ticked off at Mike. I knew I had to support what he had told Michael, but I had been looking forward to my first trick-or-treating as a mom! Thinking back on that time now, with ten years of perspective, I realize how insignificant the issue was. But it certainly felt fight-worthy in the moment!

That said, some disputes are definitely worth hashing out. Two parenting topics that Mike and I often disagree on are media choices and how many activities the boys should be involved in. We continue to work on finding common ground for these issues because they are critical to building our boys' character and maintaining a strong family. Mike and I remind each other, even as we disagree, that we are on the same team and share the same ultimate goal of raising godly men of character. We are unified in the desire to be a strong parenting team, and we recognize the value of addressing these difficult issues together.

Many parenting conflicts, however, are rooted in stubbornness, ego, and clinging to your own agenda rather than a sincere concern about what is best for your children. A good way to determine what is worth fighting for is to ask yourself questions like "Why is this issue so important to me?" and "Will this decision really matter a year from now?"

Just as humility and discernment can foster a united front, so can a shared commitment to keep learning and gaining wisdom together. The book of Proverbs repeatedly highlights the importance of seeking wisdom and accepting words of counsel. In fact, according to Proverbs 12:15, a teachable spirit is the main characteristic of a wise person: "The way of a fool seems right to him, but a wise man listens to advice."

Even though my job with Focus on the Family is to give parenting advice, I still need to be growing with Mike. I don't want to be the parenting expert in our family. I want to learn alongside my husband. Besides, the moment my heart is closed to wise counsel, I will be a very well-educated fool!

Even though my job is to give parenting advice, I don't want to be the parenting expert in our family. I want to learn alongside my husband.

BE READY TO ADAPT

Parenting will continually throw you new challenges. Most couples react to those new parenting challenges by drawing on their own childhood experiences: "My dad handled it this way, and I turned out okay." Instead of that approach, be proactive as a parenting team and seek wisdom together. If you have a twelve-year-old, it's time to delve into resources that teach about raising a teen. If you discover that your daughter has a learning disability, start researching how to help her.

When you learn together, neither of you is in the position of the expert. You are both looking toward an external source of wisdom, whether it is a book, a speaker, a radio program, or a counselor. Learning together also helps you find principles and strategies that you can agree on and refer to when conflict does arise.

PRAY TOGETHER

The best source of wisdom for parenting is our heavenly Father. Not only is He the God of all wisdom who knows every trial and challenge your kids will ever face, but He loves your children more than you ever could. No wonder nothing will unify you in parenting like seeking the Lord together. When you get on your knees as a couple, the Lord will grant you the *humility* to submit to each other, the *discernment* to know what issues are important, and the *wisdom* to guide you through every parenting challenge.

One of the most precious gifts you can give your children is the blessing of being parented by two people who love each other. Do you know how rare that is in today's family climate? God longs for you and your spouse to be unified in Him as you parent.

After fourteen years of parenthood, I cannot imagine this journey without Mike. Yes, God's grace and strength will sustain the single parent. However, God's provision for my children and me at this time is my husband. Do our differences sometimes still drive me crazy? Yes, of course! But when I take a moment to evaluate the beauty of a mom and dad so different, but truly becoming a team, my heart is grateful to our Lord who holds all things together.

1. Larry Burkett, *How to Manage Your Money* (Chicago, IL: Moody, 2000), 117.

Dr. Juli Slattery is a widely known clinical psychologist, author, speaker, and broadcast media professional. After cohosting Focus on the Family's international radio and television outreaches for several years, she joined Linda Dillow in founding Authentic Intimacy, a ministry designed to help women grow closer to God and improve their relationships with their husbands by understanding their dynamic role in marriage. Her commitment to biblical principles, relatable style, and quick wit have made her a highly-sought-after speaker to women's groups in the US and abroad. Juli's books include Finding the Hero in Your Husband, No More Headaches, Guilt-Free Motherhood, *and* Beyond the Masquerade. *Her award-winning column* Java with Juli *runs in* Thriving Family Magazine. *Juli has appeared in* USA Today *and the* New York Times *and has been heard on radio networks throughout the world.*

She and her husband, Mike, have been married for eighteen years. They are raising their three boys in Colorado Springs, where Juli can be found playing in the mountains and trying to manage her addiction to soy lattes.

17

The Truth Concerning Children—and the Truth Concerning Marriage

John Rosemond

The greatest advice I ever received about parenting—and marriage and family—was when our second child, Amy, was on her way. My wife, Willie, said, "We are not going to make this child the center of our lives. This child is going to adapt to *us*, not the other way around."

What a radical notion in 1972!

I was one year out of graduate school, where I had been brainwashed to believe that for a child to be emotionally healthy, the family had to be child-centered. All of the heavy hitters in the field of psychology were saying so; therefore, I thought it had to be true. After all, they knew everything there was to know about human beings and how to live a good life, didn't they?

Those experts also said that the family should operate as a democracy, with even young children having an equal say in family decisions like how to spend money and where to go on vacation. Willie and I had done exactly that with our first child, Eric. In 1972 he was three years old, and he'd already had the supposed benefit of sitting center stage for three years in our very democratic family.

Did I mention that my son was the absolutely worst behaved three-year-old I've ever seen, even in my counseling office?

THE PROBLEM WITH PSYCHOLOGY

And Eric's behavior wasn't his fault; it was ours. Because we paid so much attention to him, he paid virtually no attention to us. Because we obeyed him, he saw no reason to obey us. Because we constantly did things for him, he would not do anything we asked—and we *asked*, but oh-so obsequiously. Because we spent all of our parenting energy trying to please Eric, he did not feel any obligation to try to please us. And when we . . . uh . . . disobeyed or failed to please him properly or quickly enough, he threw wild tantrums that would go on and on and on and on until we obeyed or figured out how to properly please him.

All of this was happening because I had believed that psychologists knew what they were talking about; that capital letters after one's name meant he or she was smart and wise and knowing. Now, some forty years later, I believe that psychology—my ostensible profession—has caused more problems for American parents than it will ever be able to solve, if it even knew how, which it doesn't. Why? Because even the most expensive and prestigious education in psychology does not clarify one's understanding of the Truth Concerning Children; an education in psychology confuses, blurs, complicates, obscures, and just plain-old bamboozles that very simple and virtually self-evident Truth about what kids need.

THE TRUTH CONCERNING CHILDREN

If you want the Truth Concerning Children, go to the Bible. God tells The Truth, The Whole Truth, and Nothing But The Truth. Psychologists are humans, and humans, well, we tend to say what is in our own best interest. It was in the interest of psychologists to say the things they said (and are still saying) about children. Those things have transformed childrearing—something that our great-grandparents, pre-1960, did without drama—into the single most stressful responsibility in an adult's life. And the more difficult childrearing—now called *parenting*—became, the more parents sought out the advice of psychologists (and helped them afford their country club memberships). So, why should they tell The Truth Concerning Children, even if they knew it?

THE TRUTH CONCERNING MARRIAGE

Likewise, if you want to know the Truth Concerning Marriage, go to the Bible (or ask Willie). In Genesis 2:24, the Lord God puts male and female together in a binding relationship—He creates marriage—saying, "They will become one flesh." Not one flesh until children do them part, but one flesh—on the same page, of like mind, in agreement, united they stand—forever and ever. Amen!

Children are not supposed to sit, stand, or sleep between their parents. For example, in the car children should sit in the backseat, and Mommy should not sit with them, keeping them company. She should sit up front with her husband. The properly functioning family is not a democracy. It's a benevolent dictatorship. Parents tell, and children should do as they are told. It's very simple. No psychology required. Just plain old-fashioned common sense.

In a truly healthy family, the female adult spends at least 80 percent of her time occupying the role of wife, and the male adult spends at least 80 percent of his time occupying the role of husband. The roles of father and mother are secondary; furthermore, they are temporary. When the parenting roles become primary, husband and wife begin to fade away, like the Cheshire Cat in *Alice in Wonderland.* Under those circumstances, God's instructions, set forth so clearly and succinctly in Genesis 2:24, are violated. Here's a fact: You cannot violate so much as *one* of God's instructions without bringing down a mess of trouble on your head.

MISPLACED PRIORITIES

One reason why—maybe the single biggest reason why—today's parents are experiencing so much drama, stress, anxiety, worry, anger, resentment, and guilt in the course of raising children is that they do not occupy the husband and wife roles 80 percent of the time. In fact, if my parent polls are accurate (and the consistency of the results suggests they are), it's the other way around. Overwhelmingly, today's parents occupy their role as father or mother 80 to 90 percent of the time.

What does that mean? It means they pay entirely too much attention to, and do entirely too much for, their children. It means husbands and wives *talk* more to their kids than they talk to each other, *do* more for the kids than they do for each other, *act* more interested in the kids than in each other, *spend more time* with the kids than with each other, and so on. It means that husbands and wives have misplaced their priorities.

The result is children who do not pay adequate attention to their parents, do not readily obey them with willing hearts, and do not feel any meaningful obligation to them. After all, the only people in the family who are acting as if they are obligated to anyone else are . . . the parents. And children are fine with that.

Ironically, however, children aren't *happy* with that. The research is unequivocal: the happiest kids are also the most obedient kids. So in the child-centered family, the kids aren't really happy—not as happy as they have a right to be at least—because obeying parents is not a priority. But kids in a child-centered family are fine with the arrangement because they have power, and power is intoxicating. Have you ever noticed that intoxicated people think they're happy when it's perfectly obvious to everyone else that they really aren't?

In the child-centered family, the kids aren't really happy because obeying parents is not a priority. But kids in a child-centered family are fine with the arrangement because they have power, and power is intoxicating.

THE TRUE FOUNDATION OF THE FAMILY

Think about it. God told His first children to be of one flesh in the second chapter of His Book. The second chapter! That instruction, therefore, must be fundamental. If you are building a house and the foundation is not solid and sturdy, then the house will develop cracks and leaks, windows will break, and bugs will get in and start eating parts of it. Eventually, the house will not be livable.

The same is true of a family, the foundation of which is the marriage. Some people stay married out of habit. That's not a good reason. God wants our marriages to be vibrant places that people *want* to stay in all of their lives. That outcome is almost guaranteed if husband and wife are giving 80 percent of their time and energy to their marriage. And that kind of marriage will, at the same time, serve as a strong foundation upon which children can build strong character.

They can then go out into a world that is increasingly in need of people of strong character.

In addition, there is nothing—make that NOTHING!—that provides children with a greater sense of security than knowing that their parents' relationship is solid and will endure no matter what. The security provided to them by the strength of their parents' relationship will free them to become their own people. They will entertain themselves. They will solve the greater share of their own problems. What a blessing to all concerned!

ABIDING COMMITMENT TO MARRIAGE

So, Willie laid down the law before Amy was born, and her doing so made all the difference. We are married today—forty-one years later and forty-four years total—because of that wise declaration. Oh, there have been the usual ups and downs. Being marriage partners first and parents second doesn't make a family or a marriage problem-free. There's no such thing as problem-free anything in this broken world. But when problems arise, it sure is comforting to know that your marriage is going to endure, no matter what.

A husband's and a wife's abiding commitment to each other also gives the children permission to emancipate and stay emancipated. Under those circumstances, the child knows her absence creates no vacuum, that Mom and Dad do not depend on her presence to feel as if their lives have meaning, and that they will be there for her whenever the need arises. One of the greatest gifts you can give your kids is making it completely unnecessary for them, as adults, to have to choose which of you to visit at Christmas.

Family psychologist John Rosemond has worked with children, parents, and families since 1971. Presently he devotes his time to speaking and writing. John is syndicated in approximately 225 newspapers nationwide and has written eleven best-selling parenting books. He's known for his sound advice, humor, and relaxed, engaging style. John and his wife, Willie, have been married more than forty years and have two children and seven grandchildren. They make their home in Gastonia, North Carolina.

18

The Greatest of These Is Love

Stormie Omartian

When our two children were younger, one of them was the angelic one who you would never expect to do anything wrong, and the other was the challenging one whose amazing creativity enabled him to discover new ways to do things you never dreamed of telling a child he shouldn't do. It was not a matter of *if* he would do something wrong, but *what it would be this time*. We couldn't imagine.

Both of our children are adults now and, by the time you read this, will be married to the wonderful person each is engaged to. They have planned their respective weddings to happen within a few months of each other—the first occurring in just a couple weeks of this writing. Barring anything terrible, my children will soon be wed, and all concerned will be rejoicing and breathing a sigh of relief. But I digress . . .

The story I want to share is about the angelic child who, when she was in her teens, did something that she knew not to do. So as not to embarrass my daughter, I won't tell you what she did, but let me put it this way: no parent on earth would be pleased about it. And every parent surely has said to their child at some point, "Don't do that."

FINDING SEEDS OF REBELLION

I had been sensing something in my daughter's attitude that I didn't like, and I had called her on it a number of times. Parents have a great and God-given ability to sniff out even the smallest seed of rebellion no matter how undeveloped it is at the moment. But I prayed to find hard evidence and not just have to rely on my suspicions.

One weekday morning my husband, Michael, and I were home alone when a parent from our daughter's class at school called me. She told me something she had heard from her own child about our little angel. This woman was a godly and credible person who we had known for quite some time, and we were certain she had the best interests of our child at heart. We had no reason to doubt her.

She told us that our child had done something very disappointing, and we were angry about it. Perhaps *furious* is a more accurate word. Michael and I were going to have strong words and a plan for punishment ready when we next saw our daughter. After all, she knew better. She had been raised to never violate biblical standards of conduct. Yet she had deliberately done so. *What* had she been thinking?

As Michael and I were discussing what we would say to express our anger and what the consequences for her actions would be, there was an unexpected knock at our front door. Our pastor had stopped by to talk to us. To this day I don't know the actual reason he came over; we never asked him. But I believe God sent him for that specific time and occasion.

From the moment he entered our house, he knew something was wrong, so we told him what we had just learned about our daughter. We expressed how upset we were and what we planned to do about it. We asked him to pray with us that our words would have a great impact on her.

REDIRECT YOUR ANGER

The pastor listened to us for a few minutes, and then he calmly instructed us. His direction came in such a clear way we knew his words were from the Lord, for we certainly never would have thought of the idea ourselves—especially at that moment.

His words went something like this: "I know you are angry at your teenager, and understandably so. But you must redirect your anger at the enemy who has lured her and wants to destroy her life. Rather than taking your anger out on her, you must show your daughter great love. Whatever you say must be said in love. Not the kind of spineless love that says, 'It's okay. Everybody does that. No big deal.

We love you anyway.' But rather the kind of strong love that communicates, 'We know you have done wrong, and we love you too much to let you get away with it and keep going down this path.'"

Anger forces greater rebellion and can end up breaking down family bonds.

Michael and I thought soberly about what our pastor said, mentally bringing to a halt and reversing our planned course of action. The pastor continued:

> Your anger at her will not make things better. She is going to feel bad enough that God revealed it to you and that you know all about it. If you unleash your fury, she may go out and do something like this again—or something even worse. I've seen this kind of thing happen in families far too often. The anger forces greater rebellion and can end up breaking down family bonds. The love of God for her—demonstrated through the two of you—will draw her back on the path God has for her and away from the temptation of the enemy. This could be a turning point in her life that will bring her closer to the Lord. She must wholeheartedly confess and repent of what she has done before Him so she

can be completely restored. Your anger expressed toward her can keep that from happening.

My husband and I immediately caught the vision. We knew that we had just heard a message straight from the heart of God. The three of us prayed about the situation, and the words our pastor prayed over us anchored the mercy and love of God even more firmly in our hearts. We knew God would give us the right words to say and His Spirit of conviction would attend them. We prayed that our daughter's heart would be open to receiving what we said, to what God would say through us. As we were praying, the love of God swelling within us actually dissipated our anger. Well . . . at least most of it. What still remained we kept to ourselves.

LOVE IS MORE POWERFUL THAN ANGER

When Michael and I saw our daughter again a short time later, we confronted her in love. We didn't know what to expect when we faced her, but to our relief it was everything we had hoped it would be. We said, "God has revealed to us that you have disobeyed the rules, and we love you too much to let you get away with it and continue down the wrong path that will cut off the blessings God has for your life." She readily admitted everything and received our words with deep humility. She was embarrassed about being discovered, of course, but she was also truly repentant. We were relieved and grateful.

The myth that she was an angel had been dispelled, but something more substantial had replaced it. We saw our daughter as a child firmly established in God's kingdom and standing on a secure foundation of His love. The immediate changes in her led her to a deeper relationship with the Lord. She completed a time of good counseling with the pastor as well, and that did much to reinforce and solidify her walk with God.

This was years ago, but I see the fruit of that experience proving every day that God used the entire incident for good because He enabled us—through our pastor—to respond in the right way. Not only did our daughter never do anything like that again, but she was truly changed because of it. And that day we learned that when it comes to raising children, love is far more powerful than anger. Our kids don't need a wishy-washy love that says, "It's okay to sin because we love you," but rather a strong and powerful God-inspired love that says, "We love you too much to tolerate sin in your life." I saw my daughter's miraculous transformation with my own eyes, and I believe it was the greatest lesson I ever learned as a parent. It affected all I did from then on, and I know it was a turning point in each of our lives.

Stormie Omartian is the best-selling author of The Power of a Praying . . . *series. In addition, she and her husband, Michael, have written hundreds of songs. The Omartians have been married for more than thirty-five years and have three grown children. You can visit her website at www.stormieomartian.com.*

19

Be the Parent!

Mark and Jill Savage

The best parenting advice we ever received came from a husband and wife who mentored us in our parenting. Although our children were just preschoolers at the time, we appreciated Loren and Deanna's parenting skills as we watched them raise their teenagers.

We were having trouble putting our kids, ages five and two, to bed. No sooner would we turn off the light than the game would begin: *I'm thirsty . . . Mommy, I'm scared . . . Daddy, I can't go to sleep.* We would take turns dealing with their requests, often taking them back to bed—a routine that would take thirty to forty-five minutes every night.

Out of frustration, we asked Loren and Deanna to come over one evening to witness the challenge and to help us figure out how to better handle the situation. We enjoyed dessert together and then began our nightly bedtime routine: brush teeth, story, prayers, lights out. Right on cue, our little jack-in-the-boxes started popping out of the bedroom with their requests.

Loren and Deanna watched the bedtime battle play out. They patiently waited for us to handle each request, be firm, get frustrated and angry, and become totally exhausted by the whole situation. When things finally seemed quiet in the bedroom, we asked them for their wisdom. They were kind and compassionate—and completely honest. "Mark and Jill, we want to encourage you. You are very attentive, caring parents. However, the issue here is really about who is in charge. When it comes to bedtime, your children are in charge. They are leading you. You need to lead them. It's time for you to be the parents."

That day we learned that we were great at making threats, but pitiful at follow-through. We realized we were allowing our eventual anger to serve as a final consequence for our kids' misbehavior. Unknowingly, we were sending them the message that they could push our buttons over and over until we got angry. *Then* they knew things had become serious and we meant business.

In light of this pattern, Loren and Deanna wisely encouraged us to determine appropriate consequences for our kids' bedtime misbehavior. Once we determined those consequences, we needed to communicate them outside of the bedtime battles (we chose dinnertime the next day), and then we needed to carry out those consequences.

This experience taught us a second parenting principle: the power of a parenting do-over.

THE POWER OF A PARENTING DO-OVER

Now that we had a different vision for our family as well as for how we were going to handle the bedtime battle, would we be able to change midstream?

We discovered what every parent needs to understand: there will be times when each of us realizes we haven't parented well or consistently. When this happens, it's time to call a family meeting and talk to the kids about what we're learning. We need to apologize for our inconsistencies, and we need to clearly set forth the new standards.

If you find yourself needing a parenting do-over, here are some steps that helped us:

Tell your child/children of the upcoming change.
One mom we know had allowed her daughter to sleep with her in Mom and Dad's bed. When Mom realized this wasn't healthy for her daughter or her marriage, she sat her daughter down and explained: "Beginning tomorrow night, you will sleep in your own bed." This gave her daughter a heads-up and a time to adjust to that new way of doing things.

Apologize to your kids, if needed.
An apology isn't a sign of weakness. In the parenting realm, it's actually a sign of strength. Your kids will understand both that you make mistakes and that you know what to do to clean up after your mistakes.

An apology isn't a sign of weakness. In the parenting realm, it's actually a sign of strength.

Train to the new expectation.

If your kids are old enough, do some role-playing to train them to behave according to the new standard. We did this when we realized that we were allowing our grade-school kids to mishandle introductions, especially when they were introduced to adults. We wanted our kids to look the person in the eye, shake his or her hand, and say, "It's nice to meet you." We role-played that for several days after dinner so they could practice this new way of handling introductions.

Extend a grace period.

When we dealt with introductions, we trained for several days, and then we began our grace period. We offered one week with the new expectation in place, and if our kids responded inappropriately, they were reminded of the standard. They knew, however, that after the grace week, they would receive a consequence for an inappropriate response. When we did our parenting do-over for the bedtime challenges, however, we had a grace period of only one night.

Be willing to be the parent.

The standard is set, the training is done, and the practice time is over. Now it's time to stand firm. Most parents find if they are consistent with communication, expectations, and accountability, they are able to move in the direction they desire to go.

Parenting is about leadership.

That one evening with our mentor couple laid the foundation for our being firm and consistent, it prepared us to try a parenting do-over, and it helped us understand that parenting is about leadership. We realized that evening that we were being *reactive* and pushing our children from behind rather than being *proactive* and leading our children where we wanted them to go. As we began to change that pattern and started leading with intentionality, we found we had less family conflict. That was definitely enough motivation to keep us going in our new direction!

We began to apply this concept of leadership to other parts of our day:

- If we told the kids exactly what we expected from them before we entered the grocery store, we would have less conflict. Did we expect them to ride in the cart? Is this a shopping trip where they can have candy in the checkout line or not? Establishing these guidelines ahead of time—being proactive—helped us avoid power struggles in the store.
- When visiting someone's home, we established expectations of manners and courtesies before we rang the doorbell. Leading intentionally like this made the visit much more enjoyable.

- Before our teens took their first job, we worked with them on money management strategies. Teaching them the 10-10-80 principle (10 percent to God, 10 percent to savings, 80 percent to spend) before they got their first paycheck set the standard for how they needed to manage their weekly or biweekly paychecks. By leading them well in the beginning, we kept conflict at a minimum because expectations were clearly set.
- When expecting our kids to handle household responsibilities like cleaning the bathroom, running the vacuum, dusting furniture, or washing, drying, and folding a load of laundry, we found them better equipped for the task if we took the time to teach and train them beforehand on how to properly complete the task. When we did, conflict was minimized because there was less need for correction.

As we learned to parent proactively and consistently, we also discovered that most often our children rise to the standard that we set for them. In other words, when we learn to be the parent, we become the leaders our children desperately need.

A NEW DIRECTION

Mark and I followed the advice of our friends to take our rightful place as parents. We talked with our kids, apologized for not being consistent, and set in place the new standards for our bedtime routine. We determined appropriate consequences (our anger definitely didn't count!) for the first, second, and third times the kids called or got out of bed after being tucked in. We clearly communicated those consequences to our children the next evening and, as I mentioned, offered one night of grace with a reminder of the consequences they would experience the following evening if they didn't abide by the new standards.

It took only two nights to change the pattern. We were stunned at how quickly our kids' behavior changed. Now Mark and I had time for each other after the kids were in bed, and we no longer ended every evening frustrated and exhausted.

Thanks to Loren and Deanna, Mark and I came to understand that *our kids need us to be the parents.* They actually want us to step up and lead. And if we don't, they will. From experience, however, we've found it's much better if someone with a little more wisdom and experience than they have takes the lead.

One more thing. Believe it or not, now that our kids are grown, they've actually thanked us for the leadership we provided. If you take the lead, it's likely that someday your kids will also thank you for doing so.[1]

1. Originally published in *Marriage Partnership* (Summer 2005), 20.

❧

Featured on Focus on the Family, on Crosswalk.com, and as the host of the Heartbeat radio program, Jill Savage is the founder and director of Hearts at Home, an organization that encourages moms. Jill and her husband, Mark, have five children—three who are married—and two grandchildren. They make their home in Normal, Illinois. Jill is an author and speaker who is passionate about encouraging families. She is the author of seven books including Professionalizing Motherhood, My Heart's at Home, Real Moms . . . Real Jesus, *and her most recent release, coauthored with her husband,* Living with Less So Your Family Has More. *For more information visit www.jill savage.org.*

WORTHY

PUBLISHING

IF YOU LIKED THIS BOOK . . .

- Tell your friends by going to: www.bestadviceiever gotonparenting.com and clicking "LIKE"

- Log on to facebook.com/worthypublishing page, click "LIKE" and post a comment regarding what you enjoyed about the book

- Tweet "I recommend reading#bestadviceonparenting by @FocusFamily @Worthypub"

- Hashtag: #ParentingAdvice

- Subscribe to our newsletter by going to www.worthy publishing.com

WORTHY PUBLISHING
FACEBOOK PAGE

WORTHY PUBLISHING
WEBSITE